LIFE TOGETHER STUDENT EDITION

# CONNECTING

YOUR HEART TO OTHERS'

LIFE TOGETHER STUDENT EDITION

# CONNECTING

## YOUR HEART TO OTHERS'

6 small group sessions
on fellowship

## Doug Fields &
## Brett Eastman

lifetogether
student edition

Youth Specialties

ZONDERVAN™
WWW.ZONDERVAN.COM

CONNECTING Your Heart to Others': 6 Small Group Sessions on Fellowship

Copyright© 2003 by Doug Fields and Lifetogether™

Youth Specialties Books, 300 South Pierce Street, El Cajon CA 92020, are published by Zondervan, 5300 Patterson Avenue Southeast, Grand Rapids MI 49530

## Library of Congress Cataloging-in-Publication Data

Fields, Doug, 1962-      .
    Connecting your heart to others' : 6 small group sessions on fellowship/ by Doug Fields and Brett Eastman.
        p. cm.
Summary: Provides exercises, readings, and other materials for a six-week spiritual journey toward understanding and celebrating the differences between individuals and connecting with people different from oneself.
    ISBN 0-310-25334-9 (pbk.)
    1. Teenagers--Religious life--Juvenile literature. 2. Fellowship--Religious aspects--Christianity--Juvenile literature. 3. Toleration--Juvenile literature. [1. Teenagers--Religious life. 2. Christian life. 3. Interpersonal relations. 4. Fellowship. 5. Toleration.]  I. Eastman, Brett, 1959- II. Title.
    BV4531.3.F54 2003
    248.8'3--dc21
                                        2003005870

Unless otherwise indicted, all Scripture quotations are taken from the Holy Bible: New International Version (North American Edition). Copyright © 1973, 1978, 1984 by International Bible Society. Used by permission of Zondervan Publishing House.

Editorial and Art Direction: Rick Marschall
Production Coordinator: Nicole Davis
Edited: Vicki Newby
Cover and interior design: Tyler Mattson, NomadicMedia.net
Interior layouts, design management, production: Mark Rayburn, RayburnDesign.com
Proofreading: Vicki Newby and Linnea Lagerquist
Design Assistance: Katherine Spencer
Production Assistance: Roni Meek, Amy Aecovalle
Author photos: Brian Wiertzema and Art Zipple

Printed in the United States of America

04 05 06 07 08 09 // 10 9 8 7 6 5

# ACKNOWLEDGMENTS

I'm thankful to the adult volunteers at Saddleback Church who are great small group leaders and to the students who are growing spiritually because they're connected to other believers. Good things are happening, and I'm so proud of you!

I'm thankful to the team at www.simplyyouthministry.com for working so hard to help create these types of resources that assist youth ministers and students throughout the world.

Gratitude for help on this project goes to Dennis Beckner, Kathleen Hamer, Erica Hamer, and especially Matt McGill who read every word of each book in the series and has made a big difference in my life and the books I write. What a joy to do life together with friends!

—DF

# CONTENTS

## Welcome to a relational journey!

My prayer is that this book, a few friends, and a loving adult leader will take you on a journey that will revolutionize your life. The following six sessions were designed to help you grow as a Christian in the context of a caring, spiritual community. This community is a group of people committed to doing life together, at least for a season of your life. Spiritual community is formed when each small group member focuses on Jesus and the others in the group.

Creating spiritual community isn't easy. It requires trust, confidentiality, honesty, care, and commitment to meet regularly with your group. These are rare qualities in today's world. Any two or three people can meet together and call it a group, but it takes something special from you to create a community in which you can be known, be loved, be cared for, and feel safe enough to reveal thoughts, doubts, and struggles and still to be yourself. You may be tempted to show up at the small group session and sit, smile, and be nice, but never speak from your heart or say anything that would challenge another group member's thinking. This type of superficial participation prevents true spiritual community.

Most relationships never get beneath the relational surface. This LIFETOGETHER series is designed to push you to think, to talk, and to open your heart. You'll be challenged to expose some of your fears, hurts, and habits. As you do this, you'll find healing, experience spiritual growth, and build lasting, genuine friendships. Since God uses people to impact people you'll most likely become a richer, deeper, more vibrant person as you experience LIFETOGETHER with others. If you go through this book (and the 5 other books in this series) you will become a deeper and stronger follower of Jesus Christ. Get ready for something big to happen in your life!

# WHAT YOU'LL FIND IN EACH SESSION

For each session, the group time contains five sections, one for each of the primary biblical purposes: fellowship, discipleship, ministry, evangelism, and worship. The five purposes can each stand alone, but when they're fused together, they make a greater impact on you and your world than the five of them might if approached separately. Think about it like this: If you play baseball or softball, you might be an outstanding hitter, but you also need to be able to catch, throw, run, and slide. You need more than one skill to make an impact for your team. In the same way, the five purposes individually are good, but when you put them all together, you're a balanced player who makes a huge impact.

The material in this book (and the other LIFETOGETHER books) is built around God's Word. You'll find a lot of blank spaces and journaling pages where you can write down your thoughts about God's work in your life as you explore and live out God's purposes.

Here's a closer look at what you'll find in these five sections:

# FELLOWSHIP: CONNECTING Your Heart to Others'
## [goal: to have students share about their lives and listen attentively to others]

These questions give you and the members of your small group a chance to share from your own lives, to get to know one another better, and to offer initial thoughts on the session theme. The picture for this section is a heart because you're opening up your heart so others can connect with you on a deeper level.

# DISCIPLESHIP: GROWING to Be Like Jesus
## [goal: to explore God's Word, learn biblical knowledge, and make personal applications]

This is the time to explore the Bible, gain biblical knowledge, and discuss how God's Word can make a difference in your life. The picture for this section is a brain because you're opening your mind to learn God's Word and ways.

You'll find lots of questions in this section; more than you can discuss during your group time. Your leader will choose the questions your group will discuss. You can respond to the other questions on your own during the week, which is a great way to get more Bible study. (See **At Home This Week** on page 27.)

# MINISTRY: SERVING Others in Love
[goal: to recognize and take opportunities to serve others]

During each small group session, you'll have an opportunity to discuss how to meet needs by serving others. As you grow spiritually, you'll begin to recognize—and take—opportunities to serve others. As your heart expands, so will your opportunities to serve. Here, the picture is a foot because you're moving your feet to meet the needs of others.

# EVANGELISM: SHARING Your Story and God's Story
[goal: to consider how the truths from this lesson might be applied to our relationships with unbelievers]

It's too easy for a small group to become a clique and only care about one another. That's not God's plan for us. He wants us to reach out to people with the good news. Each session will give you an opportunity to discuss your relationships with unbelievers and consider ways to reach out to them. The picture for this section is a mouth because you're opening your mouth to have spiritual conversations with unbelievers.

# WORSHIP: SURRENDERING Your Life to Honor God
[goal: to focus on God's presence]

Each small group session ends with a time of prayer. You'll be challenged to slow down and turn your focus toward God's love, his goodness, and his presence in your life. You'll spend time talking to God, listening in silence, and giving your heart to him. Surrender is giving up what you want so God can give you what he wants. The picture for this section is a body, which represents you surrendering your entire life to God.

# AT HOME THIS WEEK

At the end of each session, you'll find reminders of ways you can help yourself grow spiritually until your small group meets again. You're free to vary the options you choose from week to week. You'll find more information about each of these options near the end of the first session.

### Daily Bible Readings
Page 104 contains a list of Bible passages to help you continue to take God's Word deeper in your life.

### Memory Verses
On page 108 you'll find six Bible verses to memorize, one related to the topic of each session.

### Journaling
You're offered several options to trigger your thoughts, including a question or two related to the topic of the session. Journaling is a great way to reflect on what you've been learning or to evaluate it.

### Wrap It Up
Each session contains a lot of discussion questions, too many for one small group meeting. So you can think through your answers to the extra questions during the week.

# LEARN A LITTLE MORE

You might want to learn a little more (hey, great title for a subsection!) about terms and phrases in the Bible passage. You'll find helpful information here.

# FOR FURTHER STUDY

One of the best ways to understand Bible passages is by reading other verses on the same topic. You'll find suggestions here.

# BEING IN A SMALL GROUP

You probably have enough casual or superficial friendships and don't need to waste your time cultivating more. To benefit the most from your small group time and to build great relationships, here are some ideas to help you:

## Prepare to participate

Interaction is a key to a good small group. Talking too little will make it hard for others to get to know you. Everyone has something to contribute—yes, even you! But participating doesn't mean dominating, so be careful to not monopolize the conversation! Most groups typically have one conversation hog, and if you don't know who it is in your small group, then it might be you. Here's a tip: you don't have to answer every question and comment on every point. The bottom line is to find a balance between the two extremes.

## Be consistent

Healthy relationships take time to grow. Quality time is great, but a great *quantity* of time is probably better. Plan to show up every week (or whenever your group plans to meet), even when you don't feel like it. With only six sessions per book, if you miss just two meetings you'll have missed 33 percent of the small group times for this book. When you make a commitment to your small group a high priority, you're sure to build meaningful relationships.

## Practice honesty and confidentiality

Strong relationships are only as solid as the trust they are built upon. Although it may be difficult, take a risk and be honest with your answers. God wants you to be known by others! Then respect the risks others are taking and offer them the same love, grace, and forgiveness God does. Make confidentiality a nonnegotiable value for your small group. Nothing kills community like gossip.

## Come prepared

You can always arrive prepared by praying ahead of time. Ask God to give you the courage to be honest and the discipline to be respectful of others.

You aren't required to do any preparation in the workbook before you arrive (unless you're the leader—and then it's just a few minutes). But you may want to work through the **Growing** questions before your group time. Talk about this idea with your leader. If your group is going to, don't view the preparation as homework but as an opportunity to learn more about yourself and God to prepare yourself to go deeper.

## Congratulations...

...on making a commitment to go through this material with your small group! Life change is within reach when people are united through the same commitment. Your participation in a small group can have a lasting and powerful impact on your life. Our prayer is that the questions and activities in this book help you grow closer to the other group members, and more importantly, to grow closer to God.

**Doug Fields & Brett Eastman**

Doug and Brett were part of the same small group for several years. Brett was the pastor of small groups at Saddleback Church where Doug is the pastor to students. Brett and a team of friends wrote Doing LifeTogether, a group study for adults. Everyone loved it so much that they asked Doug to revise it for students. So even though Brett and Doug both had a hand in this book, it's written as though Doug were sitting with you in your small group. For more on Doug and Brett see page 144.

# FOR SMALL GROUP LEADERS

As the leader, prepare yourself by reading through the lesson and thinking about how you might lead it. The questions are a guide for you to help students grow spiritually. Think through which questions are best for your group. No curriculum author knows your students better than you. This small amount of preparation will help you manage the time you'll have together.

## How to Go through Each Lesson

This book was written to be more like a guidebook than a workbook. In most workbooks, you're supposed to answer every question and fill in all the blanks. In this book, lots of questions and plenty of space.

Rule number one is that there are no rules about how you must go through the material. Every small group is unique and will figure out its own style and system. (The exception is when the lead youth worker establishes a guideline for all the groups to follow. In that case, respect your leader and conform your group to the leader's guidelines).

If you need a standard to get you started until you navigate your own way, this is how we used the material for a 60-minute session.

### Intro (4 minutes)

Begin each session with one student reading the **Small Group Covenant** (see page 88). This becomes a constant reminder of why you're doing what you're doing. Then have another student read the opening paragraphs of the session you'll be discussing. Allow different students to take turns reading these two opening pieces.

### Connecting (10 minutes)

This section can take 45 minutes if you're not careful to manage the time. You'll need to lead to keep this segment short. Consider giving students a specific amount of time and hold them to it. It's always better to leave students wanting more time for an activity than to leave them tired and bored.

### Growing (25 minutes)

Read God's Word and work through the questions you think will be best for your group. This section will usually have more questions than you are able to discuss. Before the small group begins, take time to read through the questions to choose the best ones for your group. You may want to add questions of your own.

### Serving and Sharing (10 minutes)

We typically choose one of these two sections to skip if pressed for time. If you decide to skip one or the other, group members can finish the section on their own during the week. Don't feel guilty about passing over a section. One of the strengths of this material is the built-in, intentional repetition. You'll have other opportunities to discuss that biblical purpose.

### Surrendering (10 minutes)

We always want to end the lesson with a focus on God and a specific time of prayer. You'll be given several options, but you can always default to your group's comfort level to finish your time.

### Closing Challenge (1 minute)

We encourage the students to pick one option from the **At Home This Week** section that they'll do on their own. The more often students are able to take the initiative and develop the habit of spending time with God, the healthier they will be in their spiritual journey. We've found that students have plenty of unanswered questions that they want to go back and consider on their own.

## Keep in Mind

- The main goal of this book isn't to have group members answer every question. The goal is **spiritual growth.**
- Make whatever adjustments you think are necessary.
- It's your small group, it's your time, and the questions will always be there. Use them, ignore them, or assign them to be answered during the week.
- Don't feel the pressure to have everyone answer every question.
- Questions are a great way to get students connecting to one another and God's Word.

## Suggestions for Existing Small Groups

If your small group has been meeting for a while and you've already established comfortable relationships, you can jump right into the material. Make sure you take the following actions, even if you're a well-established group:

- Read through the **Small Group Covenant** on page 88 and make additions or adjustments.
- Read the **Prayer Request Guidelines** together (on page 128). You can maximize the group's time by following these guidelines.
- Consider whether you're going to assign the material to be completed (or at least thought through) before each meeting.
- Familiarize yourself with all the **At Home This Week** options that follow each lesson. They are detailed near the end of Session 1 (page 27) and summarized after the other five lessons.

Although handling business like this can seem cumbersome or unnecessary to an existing group, these foundational steps can save you from headaches later because you took the time to create an environment conducive to establishing deep relationships.

## Suggestions for New Small Groups

If your group is meeting together for the first time, jumping right into the first lesson may not be your best option. You might want to have a meeting before you begin going through the book so you can get to know each other. To prepare for the first gathering, read and follow the **Suggestions for Existing Groups.**

When you get together with your group members, spend time getting to know one another by using ice-breaker questions. Several are listed here. Pick one or two will work best for your group. Or you may have ice breakers of your own that you'd like to use. The goal is to break ground in order to plant the seeds of healthy relationships.

## Ice Breakers

What's your name, school, grade, and favorite class in school. (Picking your least favorite class is too easy.)

Tell the group a brief (basic) history of your family. What's your family life like? How many brothers and sisters do you have? Which family members are you closest to?

What's one thing about yourself that you really like?

Everyone has little personality quirks—strange and unique habits that other people usually laugh about. What are yours?

Why did you choose to be a part of this small group?

What do you hope to get out of this small group? How do you expect it to help you?

In your opinion, what do you think it will take to make our small group work?

# Great resources are available to help you!

Companion DVDs are available for the LifeTogether small group books. These DVDs contain teaching segments you can use to supplement each session by playing them before your small group discussion begins or just prior to the Growing to Be Like Jesus discussion. Some of my favorite youth ministry communicators in the world are included on these DVDs. (See page 140.)

In addition to the teaching segments on the DVDs, we've added small group leader tips that are unique to each session. Brett and I give you specific small group pointers and ideas that will help you lead each session. If you spend five to 10 minutes watching the leadership tips and then spend another 10 to 15 minutes reading through each session in advance, you'll be fully equipped to lead students through the material. The DVDs aren't required, but they're a great supplement to the small group material.

In addition, you can find free, helpful tips for leading small groups on our Web site, www.simplyyouthministry.com/lifetogether. These tips are general, so any small group leader may benefit from them. I encourage you to take advantage of these resources!

## What CONNECTING YOUR HEARTS TO OTHERS' is all about

*Connecting Your Hearts to Others'* affirms fresh and powerful ways to draw close to each other—and to God. This book focuses on the essence of fellowship, a value that is universally endorsed yet infrequently—or insufficiently—put into practice. The six sessions in this book will lead to the opening of your heart in ways you never knew possible. But God did. Here are Christ's ways to achieve an amazing new sense of community!

You're ready to get started!

LIFE TOGETHER STUDENT EDITION

# CONNECTING

YOUR HEART TO OTHERS'

# CONNECTING THE DISCONNECTED

It seems pretty obvious that God's plan for the church is to have people connect with one another. That's the model of the early church that we read about in Acts 2. When God's power took over, people were connected together: sharing their possessions, eating together, meeting together, loving one another. What a great scene—and so soon after the resurrection of Jesus! That day was the beginning of the church, the church functioning as God's designed it to and as model for us.

One sign of a healthy youth ministry is when many different groups of students (groups who wouldn't normally hang out together at school) connect. That's a great expression of the early church model.

The church is God's design to bring people together. It's open to us all regardless of our pasts! I love it when churches reach students who don't look like they "belong" at church. Their body-piercings, tattoos, and clothing styles may not fit the church youth group stereotypes, but that's okay. A lot of people in the Bible didn't fit and yet Jesus called them to follow him too. You're about to read Matthew 9 and see that Jesus connected with "these types" even though the religious leaders didn't like it.

As you go through this book, it's my prayer that you'll catch a vision of what a Christian can do when he or she is connected to other believers. You can sharpen one another and open wide the doors of your youth ministry to keep it from becoming a club, clique, or community of people who are just like you.

As you begin the six-week journey discovering the biblical purpose of fellowship, it's important to realize that not everyone in your small group will be just like you. It may be weird at first, and you might think, "I don't have anything in common with that person. I can't believe we're in the same group!" That's okay. Actually that's great news because you'll really get to see what God can do with all the differences. You're on the right path for a great experience. Let's get started.

# FELLOWSHIP: CONNECTING Your Heart to Others'
[goal: to have students share about their lives and listen attentively to others]

**1** Share something that makes you different from other people. If your group members already know each other well, share something that no one in the group knows about you.

**2** If you haven't discussed the **Small Group Covenant** on page 88, take time to read it together and discuss it now. You'll find a lot of emphasis in this book on honesty and deepening relationships, so the covenant points on confidentiality and respect are especially important. Make commitments to one another that your group time will reflect those values. You may want to have one person read the covenant to the group before you begin each lesson as a reminder.

Use the **Small Group Roster** (page 90) to record the names and contact information of the small group members.

# DISCIPLESHIP: GROWING to Be Like Jesus
[goal: to explore God's Word, learn biblical knowledge, and make personal applications]

You won't be surprised when I tell you no one is perfect. No one has it all together. Even you. Even the others in your group (though sometimes you might feel like you're the only one who's imperfect). Everyone has had disappointments, bad attitudes, and imperfections. If Satan had his way, we would be stuck in our failures with no hope. Unfortunately many people do get stuck.

God's plan is different. We have hope because he loves us and wants us to be in a vibrant relationship with him—no matter how bad or unlovable we might be. He wants us connected relationally to other people too.

Matthew had a lot of money and more enemies. Jesus connected with Matthew when no one else even liked him. People hated this guy so much they even criticized Jesus for hanging out with him. Matthew was a Jewish tax collector for the Roman government. He was a sellout. The way he made money was to overtax his own people, pay the government some of the money, and pocket the rest. Matthew wasn't a guy who was good enough to get an appointment with Jesus, but Jesus treated him like he treated everyone. On one fateful day Matthew's life changed forever.

⁹As Jesus went on from there, he saw a man named Matthew sitting at the tax collector's booth. "Follow me," he told him, and Matthew got up and followed him.

¹⁰While Jesus was having dinner at Matthew's house, many tax collectors and "sinners" came and ate with him and his disciples. ¹¹When the Pharisees saw this, they asked his disciples, "Why does your teacher eat with tax collectors and 'sinners'?"

¹²On hearing this, Jesus said, "It is not the healthy who need a doctor, but the sick. ¹³But go and learn what this means: 'I desire mercy, not sacrifice.' For I have not come to call the righteous, but sinners."

—Matthew 9:9-13

Terms that look like this are described in Learn a Little More near the end of the session.

What does Matthew's occupation reveal about his character and his circumstances? What clues from the text might help answer this question?

How would Matthew's life have changed when he decided to follow Jesus?

The passage doesn't say why Matthew jumped at the chance to be with Jesus. What reasons might Matthew have had?

**6** What do you think Matthew saw in Jesus that caused him to invite his "sinner" friends to have dinner with him?

**7** What did Jesus mean when he said, "It is not the healthy who need a doctor, but the sick"? His statement implies some people are healthy spiritually and don't need Jesus. Who in this story might have agreed with that idea? Why does everyone need Doctor Jesus?

**8** Reread verse 13. What does he mean by mercy? Sacrifice? What is the point Jesus is trying to make with this verse?
- How do mercy and sacrifice relate to each another?
- Why does God want mercy, not sacrifice?
- Does God's preference for mercy mean sacrifice is unimportant?

**9** In essence, Jesus is calling the Pharisees unmerciful. How were they failing to show mercy?
- Can you think of any modern day examples of this same mistake?
- When should you show mercy?

**10** In your own words, summarize the main point of this passage in one sentence.

# MINISTRY: SERVING Others in Love
[goal: to recognize and take opportunities to serve others]

As your group continues to meet together, you may be tempted to close your group to outsiders—to be a clique—which is fellowship turned ugly. A clique draws a line between the in-crowd and the out-crowd. Make a commitment to include others so you don't become a clique.

11

Discuss ways you can prevent your group from becoming a clique.

Read **How to Keep Your Small Group from Becoming a Clique** (page 92) when you're at home.

# EVANGELISM: SHARING Your Story and God's Story
[goal: to consider how the truths from this lesson might be applied to relationships with unbelievers]

If Jesus were coming over to your house for dinner, which three friends would you like to invite who don't know Jesus? Jot their initials here.

12

13

As a way of thinking through how you might share about Jesus with one of these friends, turn to **An Invitation for You** (page 83). Write an invitation to your friend to meet Jesus.

At the beginning of small groups such as this one, you should decide whether your group is open to inviting friends to join. If your group is open, list who you would like to invite and make plans for talking with them. Your small group leader or your leadership team may have already determined the group is closed at this time. If so, a good group respects and follows that decision. You may be able to invite friends to join you in the next LIFETOGETHER book.

# WORSHIP: SURRENDERING Your Life to Honor God
[goal: to focus on God's presence]

Some people have called the church a hospital for sinners. What a great word picture! Your small group is a tiny version of a spiritual hospital—a place where sinners can get healing help. God does all the big work when it comes to changing lives, but he uses people like you to help one another become healthy and strong Christians.

Share one specific way the others in your group can pray for you. Write the requests on the **Prayer Request Log** (page 132).

Spend time thanking God for the people in your group and for the unique qualities each person has been given. The qualities of your group members contribute to making everyone stronger followers of Christ.

Before your group breaks, read **At Home This Week** together. (If everyone in the group has already done this in another LifeTogether book, you can skip the introduction if you'd like.)

You'll find three prayer resources in the back of the book. By reading and discussing them, you'll find your group prayer time more rewarding.

- **Praying in Your Small Group** (page 126). Read this article on your own before the next session.
- **Prayer Request Guidelines** (page 128). Read and discuss these guidelines as a group.
- **Prayer Options** (page 130). Refer to this list for ideas to give your prayer time variety.

# AT HOME THIS WEEK

Each week, you'll have at least four options to help you grow and learn on your own—which means you'll have more to contribute when you return to the group.

## Daily Bible Readings
On page 104 you'll find **Daily Bible Readings,** a chart of Bible passages that corresponds with the lessons—five for each week. If you choose this option, read one passage each day. Highlight it in your Bible, reflect on it, journal about it, or repeat it out loud as a prayer. You're free to interact with the Bible verses any way you want, just be sure to read God's love letter—the Bible. You'll find helpful tips in **How to Study the Bible** (page 105).

## Memory Verses
Memorizing Bible verses is an important habit to develop as you learn to grow spiritually on your own. **Memory Verses** (page 108) lists six verses—one per week—for you to memorize if you want to plant God's Word in your heart. Memorizing verses (and making them stick for more than a few minutes) isn't easy, but the benefits are undeniable. You'll have God's Word with you wherever you go.

## Journaling
You'll find blank pages for journaling (**"SCRIBBLES"**) beginning on page 113. At the end of each session, you'll find several options and a question or two to get your

thoughts going—but you aren't limited to the ideas in this book. Use these pages to reflect, to write a letter to God, to note what you're learning, to compose a prayer, to ask a question, to draw a picture of your praise, to record your thoughts. For more suggestions about journaling, turn to **Journaling: Snapshot of Your Heart** (page 110).

This week reflect on these questions: *Recall fears you may have had the last time you interacted with someone outside your usual friendship circle. What made it difficult?*

## Wrap It Up

Write out your answers to session questions your group didn't have time to discuss.

This week share with the others in your group which option seems most appealing to try during the coming week. The variety of preferences is another reminder of how different the people in your group are.

During other weeks, take time to share with the group what you did **At Home This Week**.

## An Invitation for You

Remember to write **An Invitation for You** (page 83).

# LEARN A LITTLE MORE

## Sinners

When this event happened, a "sinner" was a person who didn't follow the Jewish laws. Many people couldn't afford to keep the law because it required costly sacrifices. Because of that, the term represented a financial class as much as a spiritual condition. Poor people were seen as "sinners" and outcasts in their own country.

Jesus used a different definition for sinner: people who refuse to obey the spirit of God's scriptural commands. His harshest words were to people who gave the sacrifices but didn't live holy lives. Jesus met the needs of the people who recognized and acknowledged their shortcomings. Some were physically healed. Some were forgiven. Some went away empty-handed because they weren't ready to give up the things that separated them from God.

## Pharisees

This was a small group of highly respected and influential Jewish leaders during the first century. The word *Pharisee* means "the separated ones." They were also called *Chasidim,* which means "loyal to God."

Pharisees obeyed every word of God's law based on their traditions. They opposed Jesus because he didn't follow their strict interpretations of the law. The Pharisees were blind to their own sins and saw people who disagreed with them as the sinners.

## Mercy

Showing compassion to someone who has hurt you or helping people who are in need.

# FOR FURTHER STUDY

Luke 5:4-11
James 4:6
Psalm 34:18-19; 51:4-13

# NOTES

If you are watching the LifeTogether DVD, you may use this page to take notes.

began my journey with God during my teenage years. When I first heard about God's love, I was attracted to the idea that the world's Creator loved *me*. I learned the big-picture truth that God loved me even when I lied or cheated. I had never experienced that type of love and acceptance from my friends. This kind of love is hard to understand and to accept, but the clearer it became to me, the more it became a magnet drawing me to him. To this day, I'm still learning about his indescribable love for me. The more I grasp its depth, the more loving I want to become.

I'm amazed when I find myself loving others who don't deserve it. I'm surprised when I find myself accepting people who seem unacceptable. I know what I'm really like. I'm not capable of unconditional love and acceptance on my own—neither is anyone else—but with God's love as the example and God's Spirit providing the power, we can be compelled to love in ways that are difficult to understand and describe. That's basic and profound at the same time.

God loves you; you love God. God provides the power to love others; you love others. What a great equation! It's more powerful than algebra and more fun to talk about, so let's get started!

## FELLOWSHIP: CONNECTING Your Heart to Others'

How have your past experiences with God's love made a difference in your life? What does it mean to you to be personally loved by God?

**Don't say anything out loud**; just think of your answers: Think of someone you don't like. Now think of someone you love.

**2**

Answer this question out loud: Why is it easier to show love to the person you love than to the person you don't like?

What's the difference between a casual friendship and a long-lasting, committed friendship?

**3**

# DISCIPLESHIP: GROWING to Be Like Jesus

John was one of the 12 disciples—one of Jesus' closest friends—and he experienced God's love in action on a daily basis for more than three years. John knew what he was writing about, and this classic passage explains what it takes to make a strong connection with others:

> [7]Friends, let us love one another, for love comes from God. Everyone who loves has been born of God and knows God. [8]Whoever does not love does not know God, because God is love. [9]This is how God showed his love among us: He sent his one and only Son into the world that we might live through him. [10]This is love: not that we loved God, but that he loved us and sent his Son as an atoning sacrifice for our sins. [11]Dear friends, since God so loved us, we also ought to love one another. [12]No one has ever seen God; but if we love one another, God lives in us and his love is made complete in us.
>
> —1 John 4:7-12

Three times in this passage John says to love
one another. Explain in your own words what that
means.

**4**

According to verses 9–10, what has God done to express his love for you?
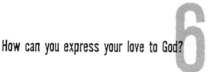 On a scale of 0 (So what?) to 10 (That's huge!), how important is his
expression of love to you? Explain why you made your choice.

**5**

How can you express your love to God?

**6**

Love isn't just something God does, love is who God is. How can you
love others as sacrificially as God has? Is it even possible?

**7**

**8** Pick one of the following groups of people and share how you can be
as loving to them as God is in practical everyday ways:

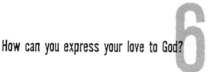 family members

   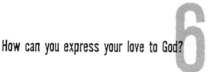 close friends

    casual friends

 people you see at school regularly (students, teachers, staff, coaches, teammates)

       people who go to your church or who are in your small group

    other _____

**9** We often love others for less than loving reasons. Which of the following could occasionally be an impure motivation for you? Explain your thinking.

◇ I don't want to be alone.

◇ I want others to like me.

◇ I like to be needed by others.

◇ I feel guilty if I'm not loving to others.

◇ Something else _____

◇ I'm not sure what the reason is. I need to think about this more.

**10** Why does your motivation for loving others matter? What difference does it make?

**11** If you have trouble experiencing God's love, what might be getting in the way?

**12** Reread verse 12. What does loving others have to do with no one ever seeing God? How does loving others help us to connect more deeply with God?

**13** What would help you be a more loving person?

CONNECTING Your Heart to Others'

# MINISTRY: SERVING Others in Love

Finish this statement: **If I fully understood God's love for me and wasn't afraid, I would want to serve him by...**

Break into pairs and share your response with your partner.

For the rest of the weeks your group is working through this book, let this person be your spiritual partner. Whenever your group breaks into pairs again, get together with your spiritual partner.

It's a normal part of group life to have a closer connection with some people than with others. If you find this to be the case and you'd like to spend more time throughout the week talking about life and challenging one another spiritually, consider using the **Accountability Questions** on page 94.

# EVANGELISM: SHARING Your Story and God's Story

Who could benefit from knowing the truth presented in 1 John 4? Write down how you would explain the essence of these verses if you were talking to this person. Pray that God will give you the opportunity and courage to share about his love with this person in the near future.

If you have time (or when you're at home), compare what you wrote for the last question with what you wrote on **An Invitation for You** (page 87). Between the two, you've got a framework for what you would tell others about God's story when you're face to face.

# WORSHIP: SURRENDERING Your Life to Honor God

Stay with your spiritual partner for prayer. Spend time thanking God for his unconditional love for you. Pray that you and the others in your group might experience the depth of his love.

Share prayer requests with one another. Use the **Prayer Request Log** (page 132) to write requests down so you can see how God answers them.

Turn to the **Spiritual Health Assessment** (on pages 95–103). Take a few minutes to rate yourself in the **Connecting Your Heart to Others'** section. (You don't have to share your scores with the group.)

If you've never taken the Spiritual Health Assessment, take the time to complete the remaining four areas later this week. During the next session you'll have an opportunity to share some of the results.

# AT HOME THIS WEEK

## Daily Bible Readings
Check out the Scriptures on page 104.

## Memory Verses
Try memorizing a verse from page 108.

## Journaling
Use **SCRIBBLE** pages, 113-125
- Write whatever is on your mind.
- Read your journal entry from last week and write a reflection on it.
- Respond to this question: *What would my life look like if I loved others unconditionally?*

## Wrap It Up
Write out your answers to session questions your group didn't have time to discuss.

# LEARN A LITTLE MORE

## God is love
Many people find it difficult to understand how God can be loving and just at the same time. They ask questions such as, "If God loves everyone, how can he send people to hell?" This apparent contradiction is a stumbling block for many. What we must realize is that God has a single personality. He doesn't suffer from multiple personality disorder. Love isn't something God does. Love is God's character; love is an inextricable part of his nature. John makes it clear in his writings that God isn't controlled by some impersonal, mysterious force called love. God *is* love.

## Atoning sacrifice for our sins
To understand this phrase, we need to understand its meaning in the Old Testament. Before Jesus came to earth, animals were sacrificed to cover (atone for) sins. Hebrews 9:22 explains, "Without the shedding of blood there is no forgiveness." Sacrifices began with Adam and Eve when God killed an animal to cover their nakedness. The sacrifice of animals continued with Abel, Noah, and Abraham. When God gave the Law to Moses, he commanded the Israelites to offer the sacrifices at a particular place (first the portable tabernacle, then the permanent temple). The sacrifices had to be offered year after year.

Then God sent his own Son, Jesus. He lived a perfect life and had no sins that needed to be punished. We, on the other hand, deserve punishment for our sins since God is just. When Jesus died on the cross, he was taking the punishment we deserve. He's taking our place. His sacrifice is perfect, so it takes care of all sin for all time when we accept it. That's amazing love!

## No one has ever seen God

The Bible is packed with stories of people who have experienced God's powerful presence, so this verse doesn't mean no one has ever seen any part of God whatsoever. Instead, no one has ever seen God the Father in all his glory. In our imperfect state, seeing God's full glory would be too much for us.

# FOR FURTHER STUDY

John 13:34-35
Romans 12:9-21
1 Peter 1:22
1 John 3:16-18

# NOTES

# NOTES

If you are watching the LifeTogether DVD, you may use this page to take notes.

# DISCOVERING BIBLICAL COMMUNITY

During the early years of my spiritual journey, I thought the biblical purpose of fellowship—connecting—with other Christians was the most unspiritual of all the biblical purposes. I was convinced that Bible study (discipleship) was the only way to develop spiritually and that fellowship was a nice idea but not vital to deepening my faith. As I grew spiritually I began to realize that connecting with other Christians was not only a necessary component but also a vital one if my faith was to develop.

I spent four years at a Bible college and three years in graduate school, mostly studying the Bible. I know quite a bit about the Bible, but my small group challenges me to live what I know. Through my small group I've experienced the love of God through Christian friends. Now I'm convinced that connecting with other Christians results in spiritual growth. It's when I started connecting with other Christians that I wanted to read the Bible, pray, evangelize, go on mission trips, and memorize Scripture. Hanging out with Christian friends gave me the desire and enthusiasm to grow spiritually like I never had before. God has used people to change me. What a brilliant idea fellowship is!

This first session will help you better understand how the people in your group can help you become a stronger Christian.

# FELLOWSHIP: CONNECTING Your Heart to Others'

Turn to the **Spiritual Health Assessment** (on pages 95–103). Name the areas with your highest and lowest scores. (You don't need to share your actual score.) When the others in your group know your spiritual strengths and areas of need, your spiritual community will be strengthened. Members can contribute from their strengths and be supported in areas of need.

How well are you connected to other members of this group? Do they know the **real** you?

2

How well are you connected to others outside of this group? Do at least a couple of people know the **real** you?

3

# DISCIPLESHIP: GROWING to Be Like Jesus

The story of the early church's beginning is amazing. The Bible reveals a great Jesus-centered community. In Acts chapter 4 we are given a glimpse of the early days. The believers met in the temple courts and in houses (small groups). Within those small groups, ordinary people became extraordinary as these young Christians grew and spread the news of Jesus everywhere. The church was born!

**3**

<sup>42</sup>They devoted themselves to the apostles' teaching and to the fellowship, to the breaking of bread and to prayer. <sup>43</sup>Everyone was filled with awe, and many wonders and miraculous signs were done by the apostles. <sup>44</sup>All the believers were together and had everything in common. <sup>45</sup>Selling their possessions and goods, they gave to anyone as he had need. <sup>46</sup>Every day they continued to meet together in the temple courts. They broke bread in their homes and ate together with glad and sincere hearts, <sup>47</sup>praising God and enjoying the favor of all the people. And the Lord added to their number daily those who were being saved.

—Acts 2:42-47

**4** What characteristics about this new community of believers seem attractive?

**5** If you could pick only one item from the list below, which would you choose to focus on? Why that one?

◇ To be devoted to learning God's Word.
◇ To be devoted to fellowship, the breaking of bread, and to prayer.
◇ To sell my possessions and give to those who have need.
◇ To go to church every day and worship with a large group of believers.
◇ To meet regularly in a home with a small group of believers, eating together and talking about God's character.
◇ To be a part of helping my friends at school come to Christ.

**6** In verse 42, fellowship means sharing what they had in common because of Jesus. What do you think the members of our small group have in common? Is it a strong quality? Could it be stronger? If so, how can you make stronger?

What role do you think the apostle's teaching played in their com—

munity? Why would learning God's ways be important?

The early church was built on small communities meeting together and growing stronger and then traveling with the gospel to other locations. Why did this kind of biblical community last?

Why do you think more churches and small groups don't look like the early church?
 Does your small group looks like it? How can the similarity between the two be improved?

With verse 46 in mind, are you supposed to give someone in need everything you have in order to help?

How would your life need to change for you to participate in a community that is committed to
- Growing spiritually
- Fellowshipping with other believers
- Meeting the needs of others
- Reaching out to those who are without God
- Honoring God with your life

# MINISTRY: SERVING Others in Love

Think about your own life. As a young adult, which of the following can you offer your group?

_12_

_____ **Wisdom** I often have unusual insights about life or decisions for my age.    _____

_____ **Experience** I've been through a lot and have a lot to offer.    _____

_____ **Positive attitude** I'm typically an upbeat person.    _____

_____ **Bible knowledge** I study the Bible and know a lot about it.    _____

_____ **Friendship** I'm a friend who is committed to others through good and bad times.    _____

_____ **Prayer** I'm someone who prays throughout the day and loves to pray for others.    _____

_____ **Ministry** I have a passion to meet the needs of others.    _____

_____ **Heart for the lost** I like to talk with non-Christians about my story, God's story, and their story to help them in their relationship with God.    _____

_____ **Other** _____    _____

As group members answer, write their names next to the terms they've chosen. During future sessions you can refer back to this page to help plan activities with your small group.

**13** What can the group do to help you enhance what you have to offer?

 **EVANGELISM:** SHARING Your Story and God's Story

**14** Look back at Acts 4:47. How can a loving and authentic community—your small group—be an evangelistic force throughout the world?
- Throughout your community?
- Throughout your school?

**WORSHIP:** SURRENDERING Your Life to Honor God

**15** Today as you end your time together, spend a few minutes in silence. During the silence close your eyes, sit quietly but comfortably, and try to subdue your own thoughts (admittedly it takes practice!). Listen for the thoughts that God might be whispering to you.

If your group members aren't familiar with extended silence, a few minutes may feel like an hour. Start with brief periods of silence. With a little practice, everyone will get more comfortable with silence and can handle longer periods.

The leader can now close by praying, "God, we want our group to..." Then each person finishes the sentence with a descriptive answer, such as the following examples:

- be loving
    - support one another
        - grow closer together
            - be encouraging to one another

Say whatever comes to mind at the moment. There are no right or wrong responses. Allow this time of prayer to help you focus on your small group becoming an authentic Christian community like the early church in Acts 4.

# AT HOME THIS WEEK

## Daily Bible Readings
Check out the Scriptures on page 104.

## Memory Verses
Try memorizing a verse from page108.

## Journaling
Use **SCRIBBLE** pages, 113-125
- Write whatever is on your mind.
- Read your journal entry from last week and write a reflection on it.
- Respond to this question: *How can I help our small group reflect God's purposes of*
    - Connecting your heart to others' (fellowship)
    - Growing to be like Jesus (discipleship)
    - Serving others in love (ministry)
    - Sharing your story and God's story (evangelism)
    - Surrendering your life to honor God (worship)

## Wrap It Up

Write out your answers to session questions your group didn't have time to discuss.

# LEARN A LITTLE MORE

### The apostles' teaching

An apostle is one sent on a mission with a message. The apostle is authorized to act on behalf of the sender. Jesus, himself an apostle sent by God (Heb. 3:1), chose twelve disciples to send out as apostles. The Twelve were disciple-learners who became apostles sent out to share the message of salvation. Barnabas, Paul, and a few others were also called apostles.

The apostles taught others what Jesus had taught them about how to live, the kingdom of God, and salvation.

### The fellowship

This group demonstrated a depth of community that wasn't seen anywhere in Jerusalem. Generosity was one of its distinguishing features.

### Temple courts...homes

The early believers continued to go to the temple to worship God. They viewed the temple as a sacred place of worship. Their faith in Jesus made their worship complete and purposeful. They also met in homes to share meals, discussions, needs, and prayers.

# FOR FURTHER STUDY

Acts 4:23-5:16; 6:1-7
Galatians 5:13-15
1 Peter 1:22
1 Timothy 4:6, 13-14
1 Thessalonians 5:16-23

# NOTES

# NOTES

# STRENGTHENED BY HONESTY

This confession feels as awkward to write as it was to share in my small group, but when my third child was born I admitted to my friends that I didn't know if I really loved the baby. I felt so guilty, ashamed, embarrassed at the thought that God gave me the privilege and responsibility to be a dad and I didn't have love for her.

My other two children were easy to love. They were six and three years old, and they adored me. They couldn't get enough of me. Laughter, tickling, wrestling, playing. Hours of delight. But when I was with the newborn—nothing. It was sad. She didn't want anything to do with me since I didn't have the proper plumbing to feed her. When I told my group what I was feeling, they didn't judge me. A few guys told me they went through the same thing. What a healing time! When I was honest even though I was afraid, I felt comfort, normalcy, and hope. Today, years later, I can't even image my life without my youngest. She's so great!

Even though it was difficult to confess my lack of love, I felt like I could be honest because my small group had become a safe place to share hurts, pain, fears, and sin. When I took the risk to share something so personal and embarrassing, I felt a huge weight lift from my chest, and I could breathe normally again. My small group was encouraging, and they committed to pray for me. You may find it hard to relate to the feelings of being a parent, but I know you can relate to guilt and the freedom being honest brings.

My heartfelt prayer is that you and the other members of your small group will create an environment where honesty is valued and sharing is safe. Take a risk in the next few minutes together. Be honest and see what happens.

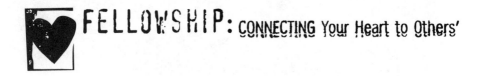

# FELLOWSHIP: CONNECTING Your Heart to Others'

What are the potential benefits of being honest with others?

What are the potential negatives? Are the benefits worth the risk of the negatives?

**Some people in this group may not like me if I tell the truth.** Respond to that statement by finishing one of the following sentences:
- I agree because...
- I disagree because...

# DISCIPLESHIP: GROWING to Be Like Jesus

Over the last few lessons, we've discussed the importance of being connected to others in authentic Christian community. It doesn't come easily. A tough hurdle to get over is feeling safe enough to be honest.

In the following passage, John tells us what happens when we're deceptive.

⁵ This is the message we have heard from him and declare to you: God is light; in him there is no darkness at all. ⁶ If we claim to have fellowship with him yet walk in the darkness, we lie and do not live by the truth. ⁷ But if we walk in the light, as he is in the light, we have fellowship with one another, and the blood of Jesus, his Son, purifies us from all sin.

⁸ If we claim to be without sin, we deceive ourselves and the truth is not in us. ⁹ If we confess our sins, he is faithful and just and will forgive us our sins and purify us from all unrighteousness. ¹⁰ If we claim we have not sinned, we make him out to be a liar and his word has no place in our lives.

—1 John 1:5-10

What does "God is light" mean? What clues do you see in the text?

John begins three statements with "If we claim..." What are the claims found in verses 6, 8, and 10?
📖 Have you ever found yourself claiming to live one way but not truly living that way? Talk about that.

Do you have a hard time admitting your faults to others and to God? If so, why do you think it's difficult?

**7** Reread verses 6–7. What might we be doing if we're walking in the light? What might we be doing if we're walking in the darkness?
🔲 Go personal: Are you walking in the light or darkness right now?

**8** How can walking in the light strengthen small group relationships?
🔲 Why is honesty an important foundation for relationships?

**9** Authenticity, honesty, and vulnerability are important components for building strong relationships. Rate yourself on the following scales, and choose one to talk about with the group. (See the definitions on the next page.)

| 1 | 2 | 3 | 4 | 5 | 6 | 7 | 8 | 9 | 10 |
|---|---|---|---|---|---|---|---|---|---|

superficial                                       authentic

| 1 | 2 | 3 | 4 | 5 | 6 | 7 | 8 | 9 | 10 |
|---|---|---|---|---|---|---|---|---|---|

deceptive                                       honest

| 1 | 2 | 3 | 4 | 5 | 6 | 7 | 8 | 9 | 10 |
|---|---|---|---|---|---|---|---|---|---|

protective                                      vulnerable

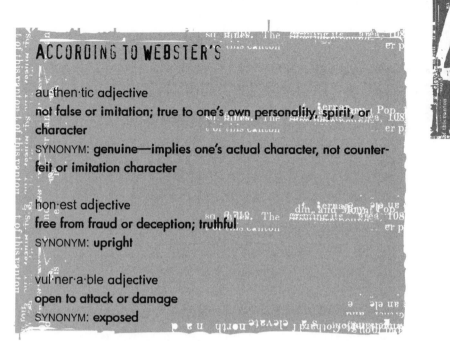

## ACCORDING TO WEBSTER'S

au·then·tic adjective
not false or imitation; true to one's own personality, spirit, or character
SYNONYM: genuine—implies one's actual character, not counterfeit or imitation character

hon·est adjective
free from fraud or deception; truthful
SYNONYM: upright

vul·ner·a·ble adjective
open to attack or damage
SYNONYM: exposed

On a scale of 1 (No one can be trusted with any information about me) to 10 (Everyone can be trusted with my most secret thoughts), how safe is your small group? Without naming names or attacking others in the group, talk about your reasoning.

What are some possible risks associated with being honest about your weaknesses, even in a community of Christians?

Honesty increases as trust is deepened. Put both your ability to be honest and the group's ability to be trustworthy to the test by sharing about an area of your life that you don't often discuss—a sin (we all have them), a fear (we all have them), a spiritual issue (we all have them), whatever. Take a risk. And be trustworthy with what others reveal.

While honesty is a good thing, especially within your small group, it doesn't mean you tell everything about yourself to everyone you know.

# MINISTRY: SERVING Others in Love

As you continue to go through the LIFETOGETHER books, you'll learn how important Christian friends are to your spiritual health. The better others in your small group know you, the more they can love, encourage, challenge, and serve you. The healthier you are spiritually the more effectively you can serve God.

Finish this sentence: **I have a difficult time serving and loving others...**

**13**

As others share, keep note of ways you might encourage them in the near future.

Remember the huge risks others are taking when they share honestly. Double-check your own responses: Am I kind? Am I judgmental? Am I encouraging? Am I keeping confidences?

# EVANGELISM: SHARING Your Story and God's Story

Many non-Christians view Christians as hypocrites. A hypocrite is a person who says one thing but does another—either calling for action but not doing it herself or condemning an action and doing that very act.

Think back to previous questions in this session about honesty. What does honesty have to do with being a hypocrite?

**14**

How does honesty increase the effectiveness of our witness to non-Christians?

**15**

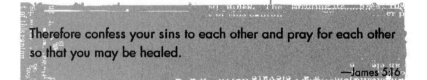

# WORSHIP: SURRENDERING Your Life to Honor God

Pray for your small group to become a place where you'll feel safe enough to take the risk to be honest. Pray for each other and the sins, fears, and spiritual issues shared earlier.

**16**

**17**

Have each person read James 5:16 (the memory verse for the week) out loud. When you're not reading, close your eyes and listen. Allow the words to penetrate your heart and mind.

> Therefore confess your sins to each other and pray for each other so that you may be healed.
> —James 5:16

# AT HOME THIS WEEK

## Daily Bible Readings
Check out the Scriptures on page 104.

## Memory Verses
Try memorizing a verse from page 108.

## Journaling
Use **SCRIBBLE** pages, 113-125
- Write whatever is on your mind.
- Read your journal entry from last week and write a reflection on it.
- Respond to this question: *What's holding me back from honest sharing about my faults, fears, and sins?*

## Wrap It Up
Write out your answers to session questions your group didn't have time to discuss.

# LEARN A LITTLE MORE

## Light...darkness
The symbolism of light and dark is used many times in the Bible. One thing is clear: Light and dark don't mix—in the physical world or in the spiritual realm. Check out John's use of this symbolism:

| | | |
|---|---|---|
| John 1:4-9 | John 9:5 | Revelation 8:12 |
| John 3:19-21 | John 11:9-10 | Revelation 18:23 |
| John 5:35 | John 12:35-36, 46 | Revelation 21:23-24 |
| John 8:12 | 1 John 1:5-7 | Revelation 22:5 |
| | 1 John 2:8-11 | |

## If we walk in the light, as he is in the light, we have fellowship with one another...
When we have fellowship with God, the natural result is fellowship with other Christians. If we aren't honest about our sin before God and others, we won't enjoy intimate and meaningful relationships. When we find out about the sin of someone else, we have no standing to condemn, since we're sinful too.

## Deceive
The deception John refers to is twofold: (1) refusing to believe the truth about our sins, and (2) thinking we can have fellowship with God when we haven't confessed our sins.

## Confess

The word *confess* comes from a compound Greek word meaning "to say the same." Confession is saying the same thing about our sin that God says. A regular habit of admitting sin to God is crucial to getting free from its grip.

# FOR FURTHER STUDY

Galatians 6:1-5
James 5:16
Ecclesiastes 4:9-12
Psalm 32:5

# NOTES

# CONFLICT AND COMMUNITY

A verse in the Old Testament says, "As iron sharpens iron, so one man sharpens another" (Proverbs 27:17). That's an interesting image because many items can't be substituted for iron. Glue doesn't sharpen glue. Yams don't sharpen yams. Lips don't sharpen lips (though some may want to argue this). The reason iron can sharpen iron is because the toughness of one metal impacts the shape of the other metal. It actually works—I tried it.

Sometimes sparks need to fly (which is a great word picture for conflict) in a relationship for both individuals—and their relationship—to grow. This may surprise you, but a little conflict here and there can be a good thing for your small group. By this lesson, you may have already had some tension. If not, it's around the corner. When it arrives, don't run from it; it can sharpen you.

An important key to a healthy small group is understanding how to bring all the personalities, thoughts, and feelings into your discussions without disrespecting or hurting the others. It's not easy but you can learn how to do it. So get the conflict started...uh...I mean...let the discussions begin.

## FELLOWSHIP: CONNECTING Your Heart to Others'

How do you view conflict? Check the words that reflect your thoughts and feelings. Explain your ideas.

◇ Good     ◇ Unhealthy     ◇ An opportunity

◇ Bad     ◇ Healthy     ◇ Avoid at all cost

◇ Difficult     ◇ Scary

◇ Fun     ◇ Challenging

◇ Other _____

When you experience conflict, how do you typically respond? Why do you respond the way you do?

◇ I ignore it.

◇ I go silent.

◇ I explode and forget about it.

◇ I explode and seethe for days.

◇ I withdraw.

◇ I get moody.        ◇ Other _____

# DISCIPLESHIP: GROWING to Be Like Jesus

If your group wants to stay together and grow, you *will* face conflict. Conflict is guaranteed whenever a group moves past the nice, getting-to-know-you phase and reveals true thoughts, feelings, and opinions.

One key to a healthy small group is learning to manage conflict in a way that helps each member become an iron tool in God's hand, one who can sharpen the other members without damaging them. Don't fear conflict; instead face it and learn how God can use it to strengthen the members of your group.

In Paul's letter to the church in Ephesus, he deals with a lot of practical lifestyle issues. Conflict is one of them.

> [25]Therefore each of you must put off falsehood and speak truthfully to his neighbor, for we are all members of one body. [26]"In your anger do not sin" : Do not let the sun go down while you are still angry, [27]and do not give the devil a foothold. [28]He who has been stealing must steal no longer, but must work, doing something useful with his own hands, that he may have something to share with those in need.
>
> [29]Do not let any unwholesome talk come out of your mouths, but only what is helpful for building others up according to their needs, that it may benefit those who listen. [30]And do not grieve the Holy Spirit of God, with whom you were sealed for the day of redemption. [31]Get rid of all bitterness, rage and anger, brawling and slander, along with every form of malice. [32]Be kind and compassionate to one another, forgiving each other, just as in Christ God forgave you.
>
> —Ephesians 4:25-32

**3** These verses contain several do's, don'ts, and a "get rid of." Underline them.

**4** What principles do you find in this passage for dealing with conflict in a godly way?

**5** When you're involved in a conflict, why is it easier to talk to everyone but the person you have the conflict with? Why can it be so difficult to tell the other person the truth?

**6** According to verse 26, when should you deal with the conflict? What's the reason for this?

**7** If you wait too long to resolve conflict, you might "give the devil a foothold." What does that mean?

**8** How is it possible to be angry but not sin?

**9** How might unwholesome words damage relationships?

**10** Which style of unwholesome words do you find yourself saying regularly?

◇ Sarcasm   ◇ Swearing   ◇ Mean teasing
◇ Putdowns   ◇ Snide remarks   ◇ Embarrassing others
◇ Other _____

**11** Conflict often results from the way we speak to one another. Are your casual conversations with friends encouraging or discouraging? Have you ever used the phrase, "I was just joking," in an attempt to take the sting away from a mean comment or to justify your language?

**12** In verse 32, Paul encourages us to be kind, compassionate, and forgiving. Which of these are you best at? Give an example from a recent event.

**13** If you were to ask God, what would he say about the way you deal with conflict and the way you speak to others? What might God be calling you to change?

**14** Do you have any unresolved conflict? What can you do about it this week?

# MINISTRY: SERVING Others in Love

Think about your family relationships. Many Christians believe that the most difficult place to be a Christian is at home. Serving your family is a part of ministry to others. Paul's words in verse 32, "Be kind and compassionate to one another, forgiving each other, just as in Christ God forgave you," are words for Christians to apply to family members too. When people in conflict know they're loved and valued by each other, conflict is easier to resolve.

You may find it helpful to practice offering honest words that build up and encourage others. First try it on your group members.

**15** Allow each person to give a positive comment about one or two other people in the group (perhaps one comment at a time so everyone gets an opportunity). Everyone should receive at least one positive. This exercise could take a lot of time, so keep comments brief. You might simply say, "One thing I appreciate about you is..." or "I like it when you..."

**16** After you finish giving comments, have one person pray for each member of the group.

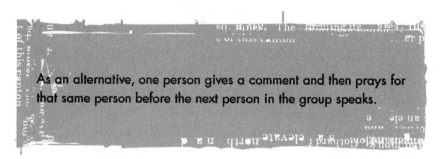

As an alternative, one person gives a comment and then prays for that same person before the next person in the group speaks.

You may want to use this exercise regularly as a way to build community within your group.

Follow Paul's instruction and reduce conflict within your family by using words that are wholesome and building. When family members are difficult, we can have trouble thinking of **any** positive comments. Brainstorm ideas of what group members can say to annoying younger siblings, bossy older siblings, lecturing parents, and so on (in a generic way, not for specific people). Give it a try this week and report back to the group at your next meeting.

17

# EVANGELISM: SHARING Your Story and God's Story

How should we handle conflict with unbelievers?

18

Does the command to not let the sun go down on your anger apply when you have an argument or conflict with an unbeliever? Why or why not?

19

# WORSHIP: SURRENDERING Your Life to Honor God

Even if you've already prayed for each other during the ministry s
ection, use your remaining time to share specific prayer requests
regarding unresolved conflicts. (Remember to protect the privacy of
others.) Be sure to write the requests down on the **Prayer Request
Log** (page 132). Challenge one another to not only pray about these
conflicts, but to also seek resolution.

# AT HOME THIS WEEK

## Daily Bible Readings
Check out the Scriptures on page 104.

## Memory Verses
Try memorizing a verse from page 108.

## Journaling
Use **SCRIBBLE** pages, 113-125
- Write whatever is on your mind.
- Read your journal entry from last week and write a reflection on it.
- Respond to this question: *How do I usually respond when I have a conflict with someone? What might work better?*

## Wrap It Up
Write out your answers to session questions your group didn't have time to discuss.

# LEARN A LITTLE MORE

## You must...for...

Paul not only tells us how to live; he also explains the reasons why. No one likes "Because I said so" for a reason. It isn't satisfying or motivating. When we understand the reason we should do something, we're more motivated to do it. Here's a look at Paul's reasons for the commands he gives us:

| Verses | The command | The reason |
|--------|-------------|------------|
| 25 | Don't lie; speak the truth | We're all members of one body; hurting someone else hurts you. |
| 26–27 | Don't sin when you're angry | The devil will have a hold on you. |
| 28 | Don't steal; work | So you can share with those in need. |
| 29 | Don't talk trash | So you can encourage others. |
| 30 | Don't grieve the Holy Spirit | He's the one who has saved you. |

## Unwholesome talk

Paul keeps it simple: If a word destroys and tears down, it's bad. If a word encourages and builds up, it's good. If you're not sure about how a word might impact others, then keeping quiet makes sense.

## Grieve the Holy Spirit

The Holy Spirit is grieved when we sin, because the Spirit knows what's best for each of us and the entire community of believers. When we understand God's grace and mercy, we won't want to disappoint him.

# FOR FURTHER STUDY

Leviticus 19:17
Proverbs 10:31
Matthew 5:9, 38-42
Romans 12:13
Ephesians 5:18
Colossians 3:9-13
James 1:19, 4:1-3

The Session 6 closing activity needs a small amount of preparation. The group leader should read **Surrendering Your Life to Honor God** (page 76) and make arrangements before the session begins.

# NOTES

If you are watching the LifeTogether DVD, you may use this page to take notes.

# REMEMBERING WHAT GOD HAS DONE

Did you know it's possible to get too comfortable in relationships with other Christians? I know it sounds crazy, but it's true. Sometimes we forget what community is all about, and we slip into a rut. Our conversations become superficial rather than guided by the Spirit. We can go for long periods of time forgetting to challenge one another. In our forgetfulness, we can contribute to our friends living lazy, passionless spiritual lives. Fortunately, when you're meeting regularly with a small group, it's tough to forget because you're with each other so often. That's a good thing.

The closing activity for this session needs a small amount of preparation. The group leader should read **Surrendering Your Life to Honor God** (page 76) and make arrangements before the session begins.

Most people have plenty of superficial relationships. They don't need more average friends; they need good friends. My Christian friends have made such a huge difference in my life that I don't want them to allow me to get too comfortable in my faith. I need them to encourage me, to point out my blind spots, and to challenge me to live for God. I don't want to make noise. I want conversation that enriches my soul.

You've probably tasted enough good community over the last several sessions that you don't want to settle either. That's great! The way to keep from getting too comfortable and to guard against powerless relationships is to stay firmly focused on God, remember his love for you, and connect with those who want the same things you do.

Congratulations on making it to the last lesson in this book. You've studied God's Word, met together for prayer, shared your lives, and encouraged one another—plenty to be excited about. Don't stop now!

Enjoy this last session. It's about remembering how great God is. Keep focused.

#  FELLOWSHIP: CONNECTING Your Heart to Others'

One lesson should be clear to you after the last five sessions: God's people impact God's people. One of the most important decisions you can make is who you'll spend time with. Your Christ-centered friends will enrich your life. Look for them, spend time with them, learn from them.

What has been the highlight of being in this group over the past five sessions?

What is one thing someone in the group has said or done that's challenged you to know Jesus more deeply?

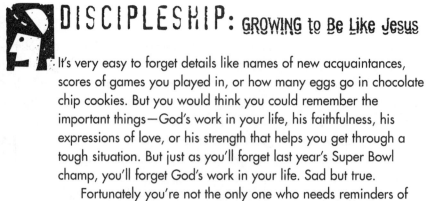

# DISCIPLESHIP: GROWING to Be Like Jesus

It's very easy to forget details like names of new acquaintances, scores of games you played in, or how many eggs go in chocolate chip cookies. But you would think you could remember the important things—God's work in your life, his faithfulness, his expressions of love, or his strength that helps you get through a tough situation. But just as you'll forget last year's Super Bowl champ, you'll forget God's work in your life. Sad but true.

Fortunately you're not the only one who needs reminders of God's faithfulness. Millions of people before you needed them and millions after you will need them too. God knows that about people. God saved the Israelites from slavery in Egypt, but because the Israelites were unwilling to trust God he sentenced them to wander for 40 years in the desert. When the time finally came for the Israelites to cross the Jordan River into the Promised Land, it was full of spring rains. There wasn't a bridge. With all the children, animals, and baggage, swimming wasn't an option. So God did a miracle. He stopped the Jordan from flowing so the Israelites could cross to the other side. It was an astonishing reminder of how powerful and faithful God is.

When everyone was safely across God told Joshua:

> [2]"Choose twelve men from among the people, one from each tribe, [3]and tell them to take up twelve stones from the middle of the Jordan from right where the priests stood and to carry them over with you and put them down at the place where you stay tonight."
>
> [4]So Joshua called together the twelve men he had appointed from the Israelites, one from each tribe, [5]and said to them, "Go over before the ark of the Lord your God into the middle of the Jordan. Each of you is to take up a stone on his shoulder, according to the number of the tribes of the Israelites, [6]to serve as a sign among you. In the future, when your children ask you, 'What do these stones mean?' [7]tell them that the flow of the Jordan was cut off before the ark of the covenant of the Lord. When it crossed the Jordan, the waters of the Jordan were cut off. These stones are to be a memorial to the people of Israel forever."
>
> —Joshua 4:2-7

**3** Explain how the future generations of Israelites were supposed to use the memorial stones.

**4** Why was the memorial important to God?

How would you be impacted if you were able to see that memorial of stones today?

**5**

Does it encourage you to hear about God's faithfulness or goodness to others? Why do you think that?

**6**

Why is it so easy to forget about all the good things God has done in our lives?

**7**

Turn to **God's Goodness and Faithfulness** (on page 86). Write down as many experiences as you can in which you've seen God's faithfulness or goodness. Your list might include events, circumstances, relationships in your life, or relationships in the lives of people you know.

◻ Share one of your memories with the group.

**8**

The ultimate purpose of the memorial stones was for future generations to know and remember what God had done. What could you use as a memorial stone to remind you of a significant work of God in your life?

**9**

What might be the next step you take to keep growing after your group finishes this book?

◇ I want to share about God's faithfulness with someone I know.

   ◇ I'd like to continue meeting with this group.

      ◇ I'm willing to take on a specific ministry within our church.

◇ I'm interested in completing the next study in the LIFETOGETHER series.

   ◇ I'm going to make one or more spiritual growth goals for my life.

      ◇ I'm going to develop some habits so I can keep growing spiritually on my own.

◇ Other _____

# MINISTRY: SERVING Others in Love

The apostle Paul wrote in Romans 1:11-12, "I long to see you so that I may impart to you some spiritual gift to make you strong—that is, that you and I may be mutually encouraged by each other's faith."

Turn to **An Encouraging Word** (page 84) and write your name on the line. Pass books to the left. Take one minute to write an encouraging word to the person whose book you're holding. Write a positive comment about the person's faith, honesty, loyalty, friendship to you, spiritual gifts, fruit of the Spirit, or any other topic you can encourage the person about. Continue passing the books to the left, so everyone writes in all the other books. (Your task is to write. Don't use up the allotted time by reading what others have written.)

# EVANGELISM: SHARING Your Story and God's Story

Remembering God's faithfulness to us moves us to share about his faithfulness with others.

**12** Turn back to page 25, **Evangelism**, question 12.. Read the names of the people you want to introduce to Jesus. Write their names here and ask God for the opportunity and courage to share with them about God's faithfulness.

You don't need to feel pressure to have them "accept Christ" during your conversation. Simply share your memorial stones with them. Let them see how God has shown his faithfulness to you. Turn to **God's Story Has Given Me a Story** (page 87) for more guidance about this activity.

**13** Who in the group will be praying for you? Who in the group will you be praying for?

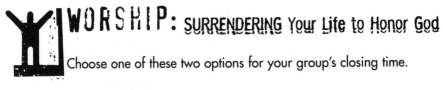

# WORSHIP: SURRENDERING Your Life to Honor God

Choose one of these two options for your group's closing time.

## Rock memorial

God wanted future generations to see the pile of rocks by the Jordan River and know he was a faithful God. Pick one of the rocks your leader has brought or go outdoors and find one. Turn to **God's Goodness and Faithfulness** (page 86). Write a key word or phrase on the rock. Take the rock home and keep it in a place where you'll be reminded of God's faithfulness to you.

## Communion

Another way Christians remember God's faithfulness is through communion—a celebration remembering Jesus' death on the cross.

If you church tradition allows communion to be served by an ordained minister or priest only, creating the rock memorial is the better option for you at this time. (Or you might be able to make arrangements for the minister or priest to serve communion during your meeting.)

If you'd like tips about presenting communion, you'll find ideas at www.simplyyouthministry.com/lifetogether.

End your time together by thanking God for what you've learned in this group. Be sure to thank your leader for investing time in the group members.

# WHAT'S NEXT?

Do you agree to continue meeting together? If yes, continue on with the remaining questions.

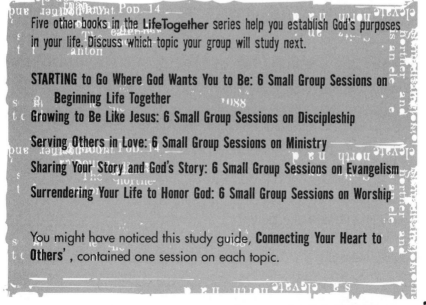

Five other books in the **LifeTogether** series help you establish God's purposes in your life. Discuss which topic your group will study next.

**STARTING to Go Where God Wants You to Be: 6 Small Group Sessions on Beginning Life Together**

**Growing to Be Like Jesus: 6 Small Group Sessions on Discipleship**

**Serving Others in Love: 6 Small Group Sessions on Ministry**

**Sharing Your Story and God's Story: 6 Small Group Sessions on Evangelism**

**Surrendering Your Life to Honor God: 6 Small Group Sessions on Worship**

You might have noticed this study guide, **Connecting Your Heart to Others'**, contained one session on each topic.

Turn to the **Small Group Covenant** (page 88). Do you want to change anything in your covenant—time, date, shared values, and so on? Write down the changes you agree upon. (Transfer them into your next LIFETOGETHER book.)

This is a good time to make suggestions for other changes—starting on time, paying attention when others are sharing, rotating leadership responsibilities, or whatever ideas you have—for improving the group.

# AT HOME THIS WEEK

## Daily Bible Readings
Check out the Scriptures on page 104.

## Memory Verses
Try memorizing a verse from page 108.

## Journaling
Use **SCRIBBLE** pages, 113-125
- Write whatever is on your mind.
- Read your journal entry from last week and write a reflection on it.
- Respond to this question: *What am I thankful to God for?*

## Wrap It Up
Write out your answers to session questions your group didn't have time to discuss.

### God's Story Has Given Me a Story
On page 87 you'll find **God's Story Has Given Me a Story**, a place where you can develop your testimony.

# LEARN A LITTLE MORE

## Twelve stones

Every country builds memorials to mark significant events. The stones taken from the middle of the Jordan would have been smooth because of water constantly rushing over them. Other stones in the area would have looked different. The uniqueness of this pile of stones would make people naturally curious about why they were there and where they came from.

## The ark of the covenant (also known as the ark of the Lord your God and other names)

The ark of the covenant was a God-designed wood and gold box that represented God's presence. It held the original 10 Commandments, a jar of manna, and Aaron's staff. The Israelites kept the ark in the Holy of Holies, the most sacred area of the Jewish tabernacle. Only the high priest was allowed to enter the area once each year. The ark was a reminder of God's covenant of love and was Israel's most sacred treasure.

# FOR FURTHER STUDY

Joshua 3
Exodus 14
Exodus 28:29
Leviticus 2:9
1 Samuel 7:12

# NOTES

# APPENDIXES

# AN INVITATION FOR YOU

Dear Friend,

From your Friend,

Think through, on this page, how you might invite a friend to know Jesus. It's not like and invitation to a party...but it is! Think personal, think biblical, think large, think small, think of what's at stake...

*this book belongs to:*

# AN
# ENCOURAGING

pass this book around to other members of the group for sharing thoughts, prayers and encouragements

# GOD'S GOODNESS
# AND FAITHFULLNESS

Make a list of ways you've experineced God's goodness and faithfullness.
Write descriptive phrases to help you recall the events. These will be
YOUR "stones" to pile in a memorial to God's provision and promises.

# GOD'S STORY HAS GIVEN ME A STORY

Review you answer to question 17 in Session 2, page 36 and your answer question 14 in Session 3, page 46. With those ideas fresh in your mind, explain how God's story has given you a life-changing story.

# SMALL GROUP COVENANT

**R**ead through the following covenant as a group. Discuss concerns and questions. You may modify the covenant based on the needs and concerns of your group members. Those who agree with the terms and are willing to commit themselves to the covenant as you've revised it should sign their own books and the books of everyone entering into the covenant.

> A covenant is a binding agreement or contract. God made covenants with Noah, Abraham, and David, among others. Jesus is the fulfillment of a new covenant between God and his people.

If you take your commitment to the Small Group Covenant seriously, you'll find that your group will go deep relationally. Without a covenant you may find yourselves meeting simply for the sake of meeting.

If your group decides to add some additional values (character traits such as be encouraging or be kind), write the new values at the bottom of the covenant page. Your group may also want to create some small group rules (actions such as not interrupting when someone else is speaking or sitting up instead of lying down). You can list those at the bottom of the covenant page also.

Reviewing your group's covenant, values, and rules before each meeting will become a significant part of your small group experience.

## OUR COVENANT

I, _____ , as a member of our small group, acknowledge my need for meaningful relationships with other believers. I agree that this small group community exists to help me deepen my relationships with God, Christians, and other people in my life. I commit to the following:

**Consistency** I will give my best effort to attend every time our small group meets.

**Honesty** I will take risks to share truthfully about the personal issues in my life.

**Confidentiality** I will support the foundation of trust in our small group by not participating in gossip. I will not reveal personal information shared by others during our meetings.

**Respect** I will help create a safe environment for our small group members by listening carefully and not making fun of others.

**Prayer** I will make a committed effort to pray regularly for the people in our small group.

**Accountability** I will allow the people in my small group to hold me accountable for growing spiritually and living a life that honors God.

This covenant, signed by all the members in this group, reflects our commitment to one another.

Signature              Date

Signature              Date

Signature              Date

Signature              Date

Signature              Date

Signature              Date

Signature              Date

Signature              Date

Signature              Date

Signature              Date

# SMALL GROUP
# Roster

| name | email |
|------|-------|
|      |       |
|      |       |
|      |       |
|      |       |
|      |       |
|      |       |
|      |       |
|      |       |
|      |       |

| PHONE | ADDRESS | SCHOOL & GRADE |
|---|---|---|
| | | |
| | | |
| | | |
| | | |
| | | |
| | | |
| | | |
| | | |
| | | |
| | | |

# HOW TO KEEP YOUR SMALL GROUP FROM BECOMING A CLIQUE

Cliques arise naturally because we all want to belong—God created us to be connected in community with one another. The same drive that creates community creates cliques. A clique isn't just a group of friends, but a group of friends uninterested in anyone outside the group. Cliques result in pain for those who are excluded.

If you reread the first paragraph of the introduction **"Read Me First"** (page 9), you see the words *spiritual community* used to describe your small group. If your small group becomes a clique, it's an *unspiritual* community. You have a clique when the biblical purpose of fellowship turns inward. That's ugly. It's the opposite of what God intended the body of Christ to be.

- Cliques make your youth ministry look bad.
- Cliques make your small group appear immature.
- Cliques hurt the feelings of excluded people.
- Cliques contradict the value God places on each person.
- Few things are as unappealing as a youth ministry filled with cliques.

Many leaders avoid using small groups as a means toward spiritual growth because they fear the groups will become cliquish. But when they're healthy, small groups can improve the well-being, friendliness, and depth of your youth ministry.

> Be wise in the way you act toward outsiders;
> make the most of every opportunity.
>
> —Colossians 4:5

Here are some ideas for preventing your small group from turning into a clique:

# Be Aware

Learn to recognize when people feel like they don't fit in with your group. It's easy to forget when you're an insider how bad it feels to be an outsider.

# Reach Out

Once you're aware of a person feeling left out, make efforts to be friendly. Smile, shake hands, say hello, ask them to sit with you or your group, and ask simple yet personalized questions. A person who feels like an outsider may come across as defensive, so be as accepting as possible.

# Launch New Small Groups

Any small group that has the attitude of "us four and no more" has become a clique. A time will come when your small group should launch into multiple small groups if it gets too big. The bigger a small group gets, the less healthy it will become. If your small group understands this, there will be a culture of growth instead of cliques. New or introverted people often are affected by cliques because they have a hard time breaking through the existing connections that the small group members already have. When you start new groups you'll see fellowship move from ugly to what God intended—a practical extension of his love.

# Challenge Others

Small group members expect adult leaders to confront them for acting like a clique. Instead of waiting for an adult to make the move, shock everyone by stepping up and challenging what you know is destructive. Take a risk. Be a spokesperson for your youth ministry and your student peers by leading the way—be part of a small group that isn't cliquey and one who isn't afraid to challenge the groups who are.


By practicing these key ideas, your group will excel at reaching out to others and deepening the biblical fellowship within your church.

# ACCOUNTABILITY QUESTIONS

During your small group time, you'll have opportunities to connect with one other person in the group—your spiritual partner. Relationships can go deeper if you have the same partner for the entire book or even the entire LIFETOGETHER series. Be as mellow as you want or crank it up to a higher level by talking throughout the week and checking in with each other about your spiritual journeys.

For those who want to go to a deeper level with their spiritual partners, here's a list of questions you can use as a guide for accountability. Depending on the time you have available, you might discuss all of them or only a couple.

### The Wonder Question
Have you maintained an attitude of awe and wonder toward God?
(Have you minimized him? Placed him in a box? Forgotten to consider his character?)

### The Priority Question
Have you maintained a personal devotional time (quiet time) with God?
(Have you allowed yourself to become too busy? Filled your life with too much activity?)

### The Morality Question
Have you maintained integrity in the way you live?
(Have you compromised your integrity or the truth with your actions? Your thoughts? Your words?)

### The Listening Question
Are you sensitive to the promptings and leading of the Holy Spirit?
(Have you drowned out his voice with too much noise?)

### The Relationships Question
Have you maintained peaceful relationships and resolved conflicts to the best of your ability? (Have you caused conflict, offended others, or avoided resolving tension?)

### The Prayer Question
How can I pray for you this week?

**SPIRITUAL HEALTH assessment**

Evaluating your spiritual journey is a good thing. Parts of your journey will take you to low spots, while others will lead you to high places. Spiritual growth is not a smooth incline—loopy roller coaster is more like it. When you regularly consider your life, you'll develop an awareness of God's Spirit working in you. Evaluate. Think. Learn. Grow.

The assessment in this section is a tool, not a test. The purpose of this tool is to help you evaluate where you're at in your faith journey. No one is perfect in this life, so don't worry about what score you get. It won't be published in your church bulletin. Be honest so you have an accurate idea of how you're doing.

When you finish, celebrate the areas where you're relatively healthy, and think about how you can use your strengths to help others on their spiritual journeys. Then think of ways your small group members can aid one another to improve weak areas through support and example.

## FELLOWSHIP: CONNECTING Your Heart to Others'

1. I meet consistently with a small group of Christians.

| 1 | 2 | 3 | 4 | 5 |
|---|---|---|---|---|
| poor | | | | outstanding |

2. I'm connected to other Christians who hold me accountable.

| 1 | 2 | 3 | 4 | 5 |
|---|---|---|---|---|
| poor | | | | outstanding |

3. I can talk with my small group leader when I need help, advice, or support.

| 1 | 2 | 3 | 4 | 5 |
|---|---|---|---|---|
| poor | | | | outstanding |

4. My Christian friends are a significant source of strength and stability in my life.

| 1 | 2 | 3 | 4 | 5 |
|---|---|---|---|---|
| poor | | | | outstanding |

5. I regularly pray for others in my small group between meetings.

| 1 | 2 | 3 | 4 | 5 |
|---|---|---|---|---|
| poor | | | | outstanding |

6. I have resolved all conflicts I have had with other Christians and non-Christians.

| 1 | 2 | 3 | 4 | 5 |
|---|---|---|---|---|
| poor | | | | outstanding |

7. I've done all I possibly can to be a good son or daughter and brother or sister.

| 1 | 2 | 3 | 4 | 5 |
|---|---|---|---|---|
| poor | | | | outstanding |

Take time to answer the following questions to further evaluate your spiritual health (after your small group meets if you don't have time during the meeting). If you need help with this, schedule a time with your small group leader to talk about your spiritual health.

List the three most significant relationships you have right now. Why are these people important to you?

How would you describe the benefit you receive from being in fellowship with other Christians?

CONNECTING Your Heart to Others'

Do you have an accountability partner? If so, what have you been
doing to hold each other accountable? If not, how can you get one?

# DISCIPLESHIP: GROWING to Be Like Jesus

11. I have regular times of conversation with God.

| 1 | 2 | 3 | 4 | 5 |
|---|---|---|---|---|
| poor | | | | outstanding |

12. I'm a closer friend with God this month than I was last month.

| 1 | 2 | 3 | 4 | 5 |
|---|---|---|---|---|
| poor | | | | outstanding |

13. I'm making better decisions this month when compared to last month.

| 1 | 2 | 3 | 4 | 5 |
|---|---|---|---|---|
| poor | | | | outstanding |

14. I regularly attend church services and grow spiritually as a result.

| 1 | 2 | 3 | 4 | 5 |
|---|---|---|---|---|
| poor | | | | outstanding |

15. I consistently honor God with my finances through giving.

| 1 | 2 | 3 | 4 | 5 |
|---|---|---|---|---|
| poor | | | | outstanding |

16. I regularly study the Bible on my own.

| 1 | 2 | 3 | 4 | 5 |
|---|---|---|---|---|
| poor | | | | outstanding |

17. I regularly memorize Bible verses or passages.

| 1 | 2 | 3 | 4 | 5 |
|---|---|---|---|---|
| poor | | | | outstanding |

Take time to answer the following questions to further evaluate your spiritual health (after your small group meets if you don't have time during the meeting). If you need help with this, schedule a time with your small group leader to talk about your spiritual health.

What books or chapters from the Bible have your read during the last month?

**18**

What has God been teaching you from Scripture lately?

**19**

**20** What was the last verse you memorized? When did you memorize it? Describe the last time a memorized Bible verse helped you.

# MINISTRY: SERVING Others in Love

21. I am currently serving in some ministry capacity.

| 1 | 2 | 3 | 4 | 5 |
|---|---|---|---|---|
| poor | | | | outstanding |

22. I'm effectively ministering where I'm serving.

| 1 | 2 | 3 | 4 | 5 |
|---|---|---|---|---|
| poor | | | | outstanding |

23. Generally I have a humble attitude when I serve others.

| 1 | 2 | 3 | 4 | 5 |
|---|---|---|---|---|
| poor | | | | outstanding |

24. I understand God has created me as a unique individual and he has a special plan for my life.

| 1 | 2 | 3 | 4 | 5 |
|---|---|---|---|---|
| poor | | | | outstanding |

25. When I help others, I typically don't look for anything in return.

| 1 | 2 | 3 | 4 | 5 |
|---|---|---|---|---|
| poor | | | | outstanding |

26. My family and friends consider me to be generally unselfish.

| 1 | 2 | 3 | 4 | 5 |
|---|---|---|---|---|
| poor | | | | outstanding |

27. I'm usually sensitive to the hurts of others and respond in a caring way.

| 1 | 2 | 3 | 4 | 5 |
|---|---|---|---|---|
| poor | | | | outstanding |

Take time to answer the following questions to further evaluate your spiritual health (after your small group meets if you don't have time during the meeting). If you need help with this, schedule a time with your small group leader to talk about your spiritual health.

28 If you're currently serving in a ministry, why are you serving? If not, what's kept you from getting involved?

29 What spiritual lessons have you learned while serving?

30 What frustrations have you experienced as a result of serving?

# EVANGELISM: SHARING Your Story and God's Story

31. I regularly pray for my non–Christian friends.

| 1 | 2 | 3 | 4 | 5 |
|---|---|---|---|---|
| poor | | | | outstanding |

32. I invite my non–Christian friends to church.

| 1 | 2 | 3 | 4 | 5 |
|---|---|---|---|---|
| poor | | | | outstanding |

33. I talk about my faith with others.

| 1 | 2 | 3 | 4 | 5 |
|---|---|---|---|---|
| poor | | | | outstanding |

34. I pray for opportunities to share about what Jesus has done in my life.

| 1 | 2 | 3 | 4 | 5 |
|---|---|---|---|---|
| poor | | | | outstanding |

35. People know I'm a Christian by more than my words.

| 1 | 2 | 3 | 4 | 5 |
|---|---|---|---|---|
| poor | | | | outstanding |

36. I feel a strong compassion for non–Christians.

| 1 | 2 | 3 | 4 | 5 |
|---|---|---|---|---|
| poor | | | | outstanding |

37. I have written out my testimony and am ready to share it.

| 1 | 2 | 3 | 4 | 5 |
|---|---|---|---|---|
| poor | | | | outstanding |

Take time to answer the following questions to further evaluate your spiritual health (after your small group meets if you don't have time during the meeting). If you need help with this, schedule a time with your small group leader to talk about your spiritual health.

Describe any significant spiritual conversations you've had with unbelievers in the past month. **38**

Has your faith been challenged by any non-Christians? If yes, how? **39**

What have been some difficulties you've faced with sharing your faith? **40**

**41**

What successes have you experienced recently in personal evangelism? (Success isn't limited to bringing people to salvation directly. Helping someone take a step closer at any point on his or her spiritual journey is success.)

# WORSHIP: SURRENDERING Your Life to Honor God

42. I consistently participate in Sunday and midweek worship experiences at church.

| 1 | 2 | 3 | 4 | 5 |
|---|---|---|---|---|
| poor | | | | outstanding |

43. My heart breaks over the things that break God's heart.

| 1 | 2 | 3 | 4 | 5 |
|---|---|---|---|---|
| poor | | | | outstanding |

44. I regularly give thanks to God.

| 1 | 2 | 3 | 4 | 5 |
|---|---|---|---|---|
| poor | | | | outstanding |

45. I'm living a life that, overall, honors God.

| 1 | 2 | 3 | 4 | 5 |
|---|---|---|---|---|
| poor | | | | outstanding |

46. I have an attitude of wonder and awe toward God.

| 1 | 2 | 3 | 4 | 5 |
|---|---|---|---|---|
| poor | | | | outstanding |

48. I use the free access I have into God's presence often.

| 1 | 2 | 3 | 4 | 5 |
|---|---|---|---|---|
| poor | | | | outstanding |

Take time to answer the following questions to further evaluate your spiritual health (after your small group meets if you don't have time during the meeting). If you need help with this, schedule a time with your small group leader to talk about your spiritual health.

Make a list of your top five priorities. You can get a good idea of your priorities by evaluating how you spend your time. Be realistic and honest. Are your priorities are in the right order? Do you need to get rid of some or add new priorities? (As a student you may have some limitations. This isn't ammo for dropping out of school or disobeying parents!)

 List ten things you're thankful for.

What influences, directs, guides, or controls you the most?

# DAILY BIBLE READINGS

s you meet together with your small group friends for Bible study, prayer, and encouragement, you'll grow spiritually. No matter how deep your friendships go, you're not likely to be together for your entire lives, so you need to learn to grow spiritually on your own too. God has given you an incredible tool to help—his love letter, the Bible. The Bible reveals God's love for you and gives directions for living life to the fullest.

To help you, you'll find a collection of Bible passages that reinforce each week's lesson below. Every day *read* the daily verses, *reflect* on how the verses inspire or challenge you, and *respond* to God through prayer or by writing in your journal or on the journaling pages in this book.

Check off the passages as you read them. Don't feel guilty if you miss a daily reading. Simply do your best to develop the habit of being in God's Word daily.

## ☐ Week 1
Matthew 5:8
Matthew 11:28-30
Matthew 18:11-14
Psalm 25:4-5
John 7:37-39

## ☐ Week 2
Ephesians 3:14-19
Romans 8:37-39
Ephesians 4:32
John 15:9-13
Romans 5:8

## ☐ Week 3
Ephesians 4:15-16
Ephesians 1:7-14
Proverbs 27:17
Herbrews 10:24-25
Philippians 2:1-4

## ☐ Week 4
Ecclesiastes 4:9-12
Philippians 2:5-11
1 John 1:5-9
Galatians 6:1-5
James 5:16

## ☐ Week 5
Colossians 3:16-17
Romans 12:10-21
Ephesians 4:1-6
Proverbs 25:11
Proverbs 17:14

## ☐ Week 6
Joshua 4:1-7
Psalm 145
1 Corinthians 11:23-26
Psalm 9:1-2
Philippians 4:8-9

# HOW TO STUDY THE BIBLE

The Bible is the foundation of all the books in the LIFETOGETHER series. Every lesson contains a passage from the Bible for your small group to study and apply. To maximize the impact of your small group experience, it's helpful if each participant spends time reading and studying the Bible during the week. When you read the Bible for yourself, you can have discussions based what *you* know the Bible says instead of what another member has heard second- or third-hand about the Bible. You also run the risk of depending on your small group for all your Bible study time.

Growing Christians learn to study the Bible on their own so they can learn to grow on their own. Here are some principles about studying the Bible to help you give God's Word a central place in your life.

## Choose a Time and Place

Since we're so easily distracted, pick a time when you're at your best. If you're a morning person, then give that time to study the Bible. Find a place away from phones, computers, and TVs, so you are less likely to be interrupted.

## Begin with Prayer

Make an effort to acknowledge God's presence. Thank him for his gifts, confess your sins, and ask for his guidance and understanding as you study his love letter to you.

## Start with Excitement

We easily take God's Word for granted and forget what an incredible gift we have. God wasn't forced to reach out to us, but he did. He's made it possible for us to know him, understand his directions, and be encouraged, all through the Bible. Remind yourself how amazing it is that God wants you to know him.

# Read the Passage

After choosing a passage, read it several times. You might want to read it slowly, pausing after each sentence. If possible, read it out loud. Originally the Bible was heard, not read.

# Keep a Journal

Respond to God's Word by writing down how you're challenged, truths you want to remember, thanksgiving and praise, sins to confess, commands to obey, or any other thoughts you have.

# Dig Deep

When you read the Bible, look deeper than the plain meaning of the words. Here are a few ideas about what you might find.

### Truth about God's character
What do the verses reveal about God's character?

### Truth about your life and our world
You don't have to figure out life on your own. Life can be difficult, but when you know how the world works you can make good decisions guided by wisdom from God.

### Truth about the world's past
The Bible reveals God's intervention in our mistakes and triumphs throughout history. The choices we read about—good and bad—serve as examples to challenge us to greater faith and obedience. (See Hebrews 11:1-12:1.)

### Truth about our actions
God will never leave you stranded. Although he allows us to go through hard times, he is always with us. Our actions have consequences and rewards. Just like he does in Bible stories, God can use all of the consequences and rewards caused by our actions to help others.

As you read, ask these four questions to help you learn from the Bible:

What do these verses teach me about who God is, how he acts, and how people respond?

- What does this passage teach about the nature of the world?
- What wisdom can I learn from what I read?
- How should I change my life because of what I learned from these verses?

# Ask Questions

You may be tempted to skip over parts you don't understand, but don't give up too easily. Understanding the Bible can be hard work. If you come across a word you don't know, look it up in a regular dictionary or a Bible dictionary. If you come across a verse that seems to contradict another verse, see whether your Bible has any notes to explain it. Write down your questions and ask someone who has more knowledge about the Bible than you. Buy or borrow a study Bible or check the Internet. Try these sites to begin with:

www.twopaths.com
www.gotquestions.org
www.carm.org

# Apply the Truth to Your Life

The Bible should make a difference in your life. It contains the help you need to live the life God intended. Knowledge of the Bible without personal obedience is worthless and causes hypocrisy and pride. Take time to consider the condition of your thinking, attitudes, and actions, and wonder about how God is working in you. Think about your life situation and how you can serve others better.

# More Helpful Ideas

- Take the position that the times you have set aside for Bible reading and study are nonnegotiable. Don't let other activities squeeze Bible study time out of your schedule.
- Avoid the extremes of being ritualistic (reading a chapter just to mark it off a list) and lazy (giving up).
- Begin with realistic goals and boundaries for your study time. Five to seven minutes a day may be a challenge for you at the beginning.
- Be open to the leading and teaching of God's Spirit.
- Love God like he's your parent (or the parent you wish you had).

# MEMORY VERSES

The word *memory* may cause some people to throw this book and kick the dog. Throughout your school years, you have to memorize dates, places, times, and outcomes. Now we're telling you to memorize the Bible?! Seriously?

Not the entire Bible. Start with some key verses. Here's why: Scripture memorization is a good habit for a growing Christian to develop. When God's Word is planted in your mind and heart, it has a way of influencing how you live. King David understood this when he wrote; " I have hidden your word in my heart that I might not sin against you" (Psalm 119:11).

Challenge one another in your small group to memorize the six verses below— one for each time your small group meets. Hold each other accountable by asking about one another's progress. Write the verses on index cards and keep them handy so you can learn and review them when you have free moments (standing in line, before class starts, when you've finished a test and others are still working, waiting for your dad to get out of the bathroom…). You'll be surprised at how many verses you can memorize as you work toward this goal and add verses to your list.

**WEEK 1**

> ## Blessed are the pure in heart, for they will see God
> —Matthew 5:8

**WEEK 2**

> ## Be kind and compassionate to one another, forgiving each other, just as in Christ God forgave you.
> —Ephesians 4:32

As iron sharpens iron,
        so one man sharpens another.
—Proverbs 27:17

Therefore confess your sins to each other
                and pray for each other
        so that you may be healed.
The prayer of a righteous man
                is powerful and effective.
—James 5:16

A word aptly spoken
        is like apples of gold
                in settings of silver.
—Proverbs 25:11

I will praise you,
        O Lord,
with all my heart;
        I will tell of all your wonders.
—Psalm 9:1

# JOURNALING: SNAPSHOTS OF YOUR HEART

In the simplest terms, journaling is reflection with pen in hand. A growing life needs time to reflect, so several times throughout the book you're asked to reflect in writing and you always have a journaling option at the end of each session. Through these writing opportunities, you're getting a taste of what it means to journal.

When you take time to write reflections in a journal, you'll experience many benefits. A journal is more than a diary. It's a series of snapshots of your heart The goal of journaling is to slow down your life to capture some of the great, crazy, wonderful, chaotic, painful, encouraging, angering, confusing, joyful, and loving thoughts, feelings and ideas that enter your life. Writing in a journal can become a powerful habit when you reflect on your life and how God is working.

You'll find room to journal on the following pages.

## Personal Insights

When confusion abounds in your life, disorderly thoughts and feelings can become like wild animals. They often loom just out of range, slightly out of focus, but never gone from your awareness. Putting these thoughts and feelings on paper is like corralling and domesticating the wild beasts. Then you can look at them, consider them, contemplate the reasons they were causing you pain, and learn from them.

Have you ever had trouble answering the question, "How do you feel?" Journaling compels you to become more specific with your generalized thoughts and feelings. This is not to suggest that a page full of words perfectly represents what's happening on the inside. That would be foolish. But journaling can move you closer to understanding more about yourself.

## Reflection and Examination

With journaling, once you recognize what you're to write about, you can then consider its value. You can write about your feelings, your situations, how you responded to events. You can reflect and answer questions like these:

- Was that the right response?
- What were my other options?
- Did I lose control and act impulsively?
- If this happened again, should I do the same thing? Would I do the same thing?
- How can I be different as a result of this situation?

# Spiritual Insights

One of the main goals of journaling is to learn new spiritual insights about God, yourself, and the world. When you take time to journal, you have the opportunity to pause and consider how God is working in your life and in the lives of those around you, so you don't miss the work he's accomplishing. And journaling helps you remember.

# What to Write

There isn't one way to journal, no set number of times per week, no rules for the length of each journal entry. Figure out what works best for you. Get started with these options:

### A letter or prayer to God
Many Christians struggle with maintaining a consistent prayer life. Writing out your prayers can help strengthen it. Begin with this question: *What do I want to tell God right now?*

### A letter to or a conversation with another person
Sometimes conversations with others can be difficult because we're not sure what we ought to say. Have you ever walked away from an interaction and 20 minutes later think, *I should have said...?* Journaling conversations before they happen can help you think through the issues and be intentional in your interactions with others. As a result, you can feel confident as you begin your conversations because you've taken time to consider the issues.

### Conflict and pain
You may find it helpful to write about your conflicts with others, especially those that take you by surprise. By journaling soon after, you can reflect

and learn from the conflicts. You'll be better prepared for the next time you face a similar situation. Conflicts are generally difficult to navigate. Thinking through the interactions typically yields helpful personal insights.

When you're experiencing pain is a good time to settle your thoughts and consider the nature of your feelings. The great thing about exploring your feelings is that you're only accountable to God. You don't have to worry about hurting anyone's feelings by what you write in your journal (if you keep it private).

## Personal motivation

The Bible is clear regarding two heart truths:

- How you act is a reflection of who you are on the inside **(Luke 6:45)**.
- You can take the right action for the wrong reason **(James 4:3)**.

The condition of your heart is so important. Molding your motives to God's desire is central to being a follower of Christ. The Pharisees did many of the right things, but for the wrong reasons. Reflect on the *real* reasons you do what you do.

## Personal Impact

Have you ever gone to bed thinking, *That was a mistake. I didn't intend for that to happen!*? Probably! No one is perfect. You can't predict all of the consequences of your actions. Reflecting on how your actions impact others will help you relate better to others.

## God's work in your life

If you write in your journal in the evening, you can answer this question: *What did God teach me today?*

If you journal in the morning, you can answer this question: *God, what were you trying to teach me yesterday that I missed?* When you reflect on yesterday's events, you may find a common theme that God may have been weaving into your life during the day, one you missed because you were busy. When you see God's hand in your life, even a day later, you know God loves you and is guiding you.

## Scripture

Journal about whatever you learn from the Bible. Rewrite a verse in your own words, or figure out how a passage is structured. Try to uncover the key truths from the verses and figure out how the verses apply to your life.

# SCRIBBLES

JOURNALING page

*finest*

# SCRIBBLES

# SCRIBBLES

# sCRIBBLES

# SCRIBBLES

# SCRIBBLES

SCRIBBLES

SCRIBBLES

# SCRIBBLES

# SCRIBBLES

JOURNALING page

# PRAYING IN YOUR SMALL GROUP

As believers, we're called to support one another in prayer, and prayer should become a consistent part of creating a healthy small group.

One of the purposes of prayer is to align our hearts with God's. By doing this, we can more easily think his thoughts and feel his feelings—in our limited human way. Prayer shouldn't be a how-well-did-I-do performance or a self-conscious, put-on-the-spot task to fear. Your small group may need time to get comfortable with praying out loud. That's okay.

## Follow Jesus' Example

When you do pray, silently or aloud, follow the practical, simple words of Jesus in Matthew 6.

### Pray sincerely.

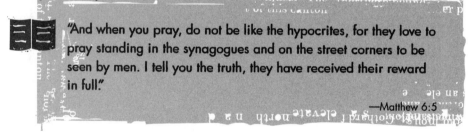

"And when you pray, do not be like the hypocrites, for they love to pray standing in the synagogues and on the street corners to be seen by men. I tell you the truth, they have received their reward in full."

—Matthew 6:5

In the Old Testament, God's people were disciplined prayer warriors. They developed specific prayers to use for every special occasion or need. They had prayers for light and darkness, prayers for fire and rain, prayers for good news and bad. They even had prayers for travel, holidays, holy days, and Sabbath days.

Every day the faithful would stop to pray at 9:00 A.M., noon, and 3:00 P.M., a sort of religious coffee break. Their ritual was impressive, to say the least, but being legalistic has its downside. The proud, self-righteous types would strategically plan their schedules to be in the middle of a crowd when it was time for prayer so everyone could hear them as they prayed loudly. You can see the problem. What was intended to promote spiritual passion became a drama for the crowd.

The Lord wants our prayers addressed to him alone. That seems obvious enough, yet how many of us pray more with the need to impress our listeners than to communicate with God? This is the problem if you're prideful like the Pharisees about the excellent quality of your prayers. But it can also be a problem if you're new to prayer and concerned that you don't know how to "pray right." Don't concern yourself with what others think; just talk to God as if you were sitting in a chair next to him.

## Pray simply.

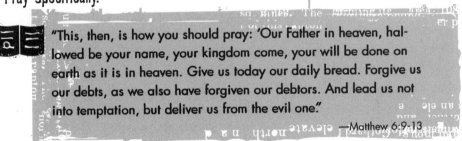

"And when you pray, do not keep on babbling like pagans, for they think they will be heard because of their many words. Do not be like them, for your Father knows what you need before you ask him."

—Matthew 6:7-8

The Lord doesn't ask to be dazzled with brilliantly crafted language. Nor is he impressed with lengthy monologues. It's freeing to know that he wants us to keep it simple.

## Pray specifically.

"This, then, is how you should pray: 'Our Father in heaven, hallowed be your name, your kingdom come, your will be done on earth as it is in heaven. Give us today our daily bread. Forgive us our debts, as we also have forgiven our debtors. And lead us not into temptation, but deliver us from the evil one.'"

—Matthew 6:9-13

What the church has come to call **The Lord's Prayer** is a model of the kind of brief but specific prayers we may offer anytime, anywhere. Look at some of the specific items mentioned:

**Adoration**—hallowed be your name

**Provision**—your kingdom come...your will be done...give us today our daily bread

**Forgiveness**—forgive us our debts

**Protection**—lead us not into temptation

# PRAYER REQUEST GUIDLINES

**B**ecause prayer time is so vital, small group members need to know some basic guidelines for sharing, handling, and praying for prayer requests. Without a commitment from each person to honor these simple suggestions, prayer time can be dominated by one person, be a gossipfest, or be a never-ending story time. (There are appropriate times to tell personal stories, but this may not be the best time.)

Here are a few suggestions for each group to consider:

## Write the requests down.

Each small group member should write down every prayer request on the **Prayer Request Log** (pages 132-137). When you commit to a small group, you're agreeing to be part of the spiritual community, which includes praying for one another. By keeping track of prayer requests, you can be aware of how God answers them. You'll be amazed at God's power and faithfulness.

As an alternative, one person can record the requests and e-mail them to the rest of the group. If your group chooses this option, *safeguard confidentiality.* Be sure personal information isn't compromised. Some people share e-mail accounts with parents or siblings. Develop a workable plan for this option.

## Give everyone an opportunity to share.

As a group, be mindful of the amount of time remaining and the number of people who still want to share. You won't be able to share every thought or detail about a situation.

Obviously if someone experiences a crisis, you may need to focus exclusively on that group member by giving him or her extended time and focused prayer. (However, *true* crises are infrequent.)

The leader can limit the time by making a comment such as one of the following:

- Everyone can share one praise or request.
- Simply tell us what to pray for. We can talk more later.
- We're only going to pray for requests about the people in our group.
- We've run out of time to share prayer requests. Take a moment to write down your prayer request and give it to me [or identify another person]. You'll get them by e-mail tomorrow.

# Just as people are free to share, they're free to not share.

The goal of a healthy small group should be to create an environment where partici-pants feel comfortable sharing about their lives. Still, not everyone needs to share each week. Here's what I tell my small group:

As a small group we're here to support one another in prayer. This doesn't mean that everyone has to share something. In fact, I don't want you to think, *I've got to share something*. There's no need to make up prayer requests just to have something to say. If you have something you'd like the group to pray for, let us know. If not, that's fine too.

# No gossip allowed.

Don't allow sharing prayer requests to become an excuse for gossip. This is easy to do if you all aren't careful. If you're not part of the problem or solution, consider the information gossip. Sharing the request without the story behind it helps prevent gossip. Also speak in general terms without giving names or details ("I have a friend who's in trouble. God knows who it is. Pray for me that I can be a good friend.").

If a prayer request starts going astray, someone should kindly intercede, per-haps with a question such as, "How can we pray for *you* in this situation?"

# Don't give advice or try to fix the problem.

When people share their struggles and problems, a common response is to try to fix the problem by offering advice. At the right time, the group might provide input on a particular problem, but during prayer time, keep focused on praying for the need. Often God's best work in a person's life comes through times of struggle and pain.

# Keep in touch.

Make sure you exchange phone numbers and emails before you leave the first meeting, so you can contact someone who needs prayer or encouragement before the next time your group meets. You can write each person's contact information on the **Small Group Roster** (page 90).

# During the Small Group Gathering

- One person closes in prayer for the entire group.
- Pray silently. Have one person close the silent prayer time after a while with *Amen*.
- The leader or other group member prays out loud for each person in the group.
- Everyone prays for one request or person. This can be done randomly during prayer or, as the request is shared, a willing pray-er can announce, "I'll pray for that."
- Everyone who wants to pray takes a turn or two. Not everyone needs to pray out loud.
- Split the group into half and pray together in a smaller group.
- Pair up and pray for each other.
- On occasion, each person can share what he or she is thankful for before a prayer request, so prayer requests don't become negative from focusing only on problems. Prayer isn't just asking for stuff. It includes praising God and being thankful for his generosity toward us.

CONNECTING Your Heart to Others'

◻ If you're having an animated discussion about a Bible passage or a life situation, don't feel like you *must* cut it short for prayer requests. Use it as an opportunity to add a little variety to the prayer time by praying some *other* day between sessions.

## Outside the Group Time

You can use these options if you run out of time to pray during the meeting or in addition to prayer during the meeting.

◻ Send prayer requests to each other via e-mail.
◻ Pick partners and phone each other.
◻ Have each person in the small group choose a day to pray for everyone in the group. Perhaps you can work it out to have each day of the week covered. Let participants report back at each meeting for accountability.
◻ Have each person pray for just one other person in the group for the entire week. (Everyone prays for the person on the left or on the right or draw names.)

# PRAYER REQUEST LOG

| DATE | who shared | ReQuest | rEsponse/ anSweR |
|------|------------|---------|------------------|
|      |            |         |                  |
|      |            |         |                  |
|      |            |         |                  |
|      |            |         |                  |
|      |            |         |                  |
|      |            |         |                  |
|      |            |         |                  |
|      |            |         |                  |
|      |            |         |                  |
|      |            |         |                  |
|      |            |         |                  |
|      |            |         |                  |

# PRAYER REQUEST LOG

| DATE | who shared | ReQuest | rEsponse/ anSweR |
|------|------------|---------|------------------|
|      |            |         |                  |
|      |            |         |                  |
|      |            |         |                  |
|      |            |         |                  |
|      |            |         |                  |
|      |            |         |                  |
|      |            |         |                  |
|      |            |         |                  |
|      |            |         |                  |
|      |            |         |                  |
|      |            |         |                  |
|      |            |         |                  |

# PRAYER REQUEST LOG

| DATE | who shared | ReQuest | rEsponse/ anSweR |
|------|-----------|---------|------------------|
|      |           |         |                  |
|      |           |         |                  |
|      |           |         |                  |
|      |           |         |                  |
|      |           |         |                  |
|      |           |         |                  |
|      |           |         |                  |
|      |           |         |                  |
|      |           |         |                  |
|      |           |         |                  |
|      |           |         |                  |
|      |           |         |                  |
|      |           |         |                  |

# PRAYER REQUEST LOG

| DATE | who shared | ReQuest | rEsponse/ anSweR |
|------|-----------|---------|------------------|
|      |           |         |                  |
|      |           |         |                  |
|      |           |         |                  |
|      |           |         |                  |
|      |           |         |                  |
|      |           |         |                  |
|      |           |         |                  |
|      |           |         |                  |
|      |           |         |                  |
|      |           |         |                  |
|      |           |         |                  |
|      |           |         |                  |
|      |           |         |                  |

# PRAYER REQUEST LOG

| DATE | who shared | ReQuest | rEspOnse/ anSweR |
|------|-----------|---------|------------------|
|      |           |         |                  |
|      |           |         |                  |
|      |           |         |                  |
|      |           |         |                  |
|      |           |         |                  |
|      |           |         |                  |
|      |           |         |                  |
|      |           |         |                  |
|      |           |         |                  |
|      |           |         |                  |
|      |           |         |                  |
|      |           |         |                  |
|      |           |         |                  |

# PRAYER REQUEST LOG

| DATE | who shared | ReQuest | r8sp0nse/ anSweR |
|------|-----------|---------|------------------|
|      |           |         |                  |
|      |           |         |                  |
|      |           |         |                  |
|      |           |         |                  |
|      |           |         |                  |
|      |           |         |                  |
|      |           |         |                  |
|      |           |         |                  |
|      |           |         |                  |
|      |           |         |                  |
|      |           |         |                  |

# LIFE TOGETHER FOR A YEAR

**Y**our group will benefit the most if you work through the entire LIFETOGETHER series. The longer your group is together, the better your chances of maturing spiritually and integrating the biblical purposes into your life. Here's a plan to complete the series in one year.

I recommend you begin with **STARTING to Go Where God Wants You to Be**, because it contains an introduction to each of the five biblical purposes (though it isn't mandatory). You can use the rest of the books in any order.

As you look at your youth ministry calendar, you may want to use the books in the order they compliment events the youth group will be participating in. For example, if you plan to have an evangelism outreach in the fall, study **SHARING Your Story and God's Story** first to build momentum. Study **SERVING Others in Love** in late winter to prepare for the spring break missions' trip.

Use your imagination to celebrate the completion of each book. Have a worship service, an outreach party, a service project, a fun night out, a meet-the-family dinner, or whatever else you can dream up.

CONNECTING Your Heart to Others'

| Number of weeks | Meeting topic |
|---|---|
| 1 | Planning meeting—a casual gathering to get acquainted, discuss expectations, and refine the covenant (see page 88). |
| 6 | **STARTING to Go Where God Wants You to Be** |
| 1 | Celebration |
| 6 | **CONNECTING Your Heart to Others'** |
| 1 | Celebration |
| 6 | **SHARING Your Story and God's Story** |
| 1 | Celebration |
| 6 | **GROWING to Be Like Jesus** |
| 1 | Celebration |
| 6 | **SERVING Others in Love** |
| 1 | Celebration |
| 6 | **SURRENDERING Your Life to Honor God** |
| 1 | Celebration |
| 2 | Christmas break |
| 1 | Easter break |
| 6 | Summer break |
| 52 | One year |

Dear Kathleen,

I just wanted to let you know how thankful I am for the dedication you showed me as my small group leader. I love telling people, "Kathleen is my small group leader — she's the best!" Next to God, you have had the greatest influence in my life. I want to grow up and love people like you, love Jesus like you do, love my future husband like you do, and be a small group leader like you.

What's amazing about you, is that all the girls in our small group felt like you liked them the most. We also felt your push. As I look back over my junior high and high school years, you loved me enough to challenge me to change. Thank you for always asking about my prayer life, my quiet times, my ministry, my heart. Thanks for seeing who I could be.

You've made a huge difference in my life. Thank you!

Love,
Sarah

Whether you are a student or a leader, when you're a part of a small group — investing your life in others — you're making a difference that will last an eternity. At Simply Youth Ministry we are dedicated to helping you do just that. For students, we've got tools like the *One Minute Bible*, that will help you grow in your faith. For leaders, we've got all kinds of resources that will help you simplify your ministry and save you time. For both of you, we have a deep appreciation for your commitment to serving Christ and loving each other.

doug fields'
**simply youth ministry**
simplifying ministry...saving you time.

toll free: 1-866-9-simply
simplyyouthministry.com

# ABOUT THE AUTHORS

**Doug Fields,** a respected youth ministry leader for over two decades, has authored or coauthored more than 30 books, including **Purpose-Driven Youth Ministry, Your First Two Years of Youth Ministry,** and **Videos That Teach.** With an M.Div. from Fuller Theological Seminary, Doug is the youth pastor at Saddleback Church, president of simplyyouthministry.com, and a frequent presenter at Youth Specialties events. Doug and his wife, Cathy, have three children.

**Brett Eastman** is pastor of membership and small groups at Saddleback Church, where there are now over 1,500 small group leaders and a growing network of volunteer coaches and bivocational pastors. Brett created the Healthy Small Group strategy and he leads the Large Church Small Group Forums for the Leadership Network. Brett is coauthor of the DOING LIFE TOGETHER Bible study series. Brett and his wife, Dee, have five children.